MW00899680

Forward

The history of Amelia County, Virginia dates back to 1734 and 1735 when it was formed out of Prince George and Brunswick Counties; since that time surrounding counties such as Prince Edward and Nottoway were birthed by using parts of Amelia. The county was named after Princess Amelia of Great Britain. Developed initially for plantation and agriculture use, Amelia thrived and operated by slave labor. African Americans constructed most of the buildings that were built in the 1700s until now. There have been many African Americans who have made significant impacts within the county of Amelia since the era of slavery; however, most of them have never been recognized. Some of the names of our slave ancestors have been long forgotten; fortunately, others have resurfaced in recent years. With the encouragement of the late Dr. Henry Featherston and the backing from my staff, my Pastor, family, and friends I decided to take on this God-given task of continuing to preserve the African American history that is laced within this county. There are many unsung heroes, past and present, who have made noteworthy accomplishments within their own lives, significant differences in the lives of others, and who have left a legacy that I'm willing to argue very few citizens of Amelia are aware of. I have done my due diligence to research, interview, and learn about a large number of them to accurately tell their story within this book. The number of hours I've spent interviewing and examining records that date back to the 1800s and beyond have been well worth it. Now, I have been blessed to write this body of work that represents the individuals whose ancestry spans back to the shores of African soil; whose forefathers were stolen from their families and forced on ships, then taken to a land that they had no connection to. Once they arrived in that unfamiliar territory, they were forced to labor as indentured servants or slaves on plantations. Found within this book are stories of people who endured the war and fought against Jim Crow Laws during the years of segregation. As you read you will learn of others who spoke out against injustices in Amelia, people who are still living within the community today who helped integrate the Amelia Public Schools; young business owners who have overcome struggles and now desire to make a difference in the lives of others, plus so much more. I honor each person whose name is mentioned in this book--for their perseverance and strength to become who God called them to be. I present to you, the reader, *The Unsung African American Heroes of Amelia County* (Vol.1). This is the first of a series of books that will honor the African American heroes in Amelia. I pray this book will give you an understanding of the trials, triumphs, and the history of those who have and are paving the way for generations to come. May this book be a blessing to each of you.

Sincerely,

Emanuel Hyde III

Minister Emanuel Hyde III

Table of Contents

Slavery Timeline

- **1619** The first African slaves arrive in Virginia

- **1787** Slavery is made illegal in the Northwest Territory. The U.S Constitution states that Congress may not ban the slave trade until 1808.

- **1793** Eli Whitney's invention of the cotton gin greatly increases the demand for slave labor.

- **1793** A federal fugitive slave law is enacted which provided for the return of any slaves who had escaped and crossed state lines.

- **1800** Gabriel Prosser, an enslaved African American blacksmith, organizes a slave revolt intending to march in Richmond, Virginia. The conspiracy is uncovered, and Prosser and a number of the rebels are hanged. Virginia's slave laws are consequently tightened.

- **1808** Congress bans the importation of slaves from Africa.

- **1831** Nat Turner, an enslaved African American preacher, leads the most significant slave uprising in American history. He and his band of followers launch a short but bloody rebellion in Southampton County, Virginia. The militia quells the rebellion, and Turner is eventually hanged. As a consequence, Virginia institutes much stricter slave laws.

- **1831** William Lloyd Garrison begins publishing the *Liberator*, a weekly paper that advocates for the complete abolition of slavery. He becomes one of the most famous figures in the abolitionist movement.

- **1849** Harriet Tubman escapes from slavery and becomes one of the most effective and celebrated leaders of the Underground Railroad.

- **1852** Harriet Beecher Stowe's novel, *Uncle Tom's Cabin* is published. It becomes one of the most influential works to stir anti-slavery sentiments.

- **1854** Congress passes the Kansas-Nebraska Act; which established the territories of Kansas and Nebraska. The legislation repeals the Missouri Compromise of 1820 and renews tensions between anti- and pro-slavery groups.

- **1857** The Dred Scott case holds that Congress does not have the right to ban slavery in states and argues that slaves are not citizens.

- **1859** John Brown and twenty-one of his followers captures the federal arsenal in Harpers Ferry, Virginia (now called West Virginia), in an attempt to launch a slave revolt.

- **1861** The Confederacy is founded when the Deep South secedes, and the Civil War begins.

- **1863** President Lincoln issues the *Emancipation Proclamation* which declares that all persons held as slaves within the Confederate states are now free, and shall henceforward be free.

- **1865** The Civil War ends. Lincoln is assassinated. The 13th Amendment abolishes slavery throughout the United States. On June 19th, slavery in the United States effectively ended when 250,000 slaves in Texas finally received the news that the Civil War was over two months earlier.

Slavery in Amelia

In 1790, both Amelia and Nottoway County had the highest slave population in all of Virginia. Throughout the entire county of Amelia, there were 11,300 slaves and only 106 free blacks. The majority of the free blacks who resided within Amelia were called mulatto, which means they were of a mixed race, and a few of these individuals were slaveholders themselves. A large number of the plantation owners within this county had substantial amounts of land, and they were able to make a living by growing tobacco, wheat, and other crops on that said land while forcing their slaves to work the fields. Slaves maintained the land and everything associated with it; they were the gardeners, carpenters, woodworkers, shoemakers, blacksmiths, cooks, nursemaids for the children, and maids for the main house. There was always a slave who looked over and tended to livestock such as geese, cows, sheep, mules, goats, oxen and other animals. Other slave and landowners owned such large territories that their property resembled what some would call a small town—everything they required was already on their land. Several of the owners from various plantations in Amelia built reputations by managing their slaves and land in such a way that they were able to develop ties and purchase property in the Deep South. The unfortunate truth is that African Americans during the time of slavery were considered property; so, not only were they purchased and sold, but the purchaser was also required to pay taxes on any slaves they acquired. Often time owners rented out their slaves to go work in other counties or states. As a result of this, there were incidences when slaves were fought over through court proceedings if the terms of the rental agreement were not honored. It was common for slave owners to include their slaves in their will so that upon their death they would be given to the slave owners nearest kin. Another commonality, before the abolishment of slavery, was for slaves to be given away as wedding presents. Very clearly, slaves had no rights of their own. African Americans endured many injustices while enslaved and those injustices included not even being able to choose who they would conceive a child with. Through instances of rape, countless slave owners fathered children with their female slaves—sometimes raping them in front of their husbands. There were a sizeable amount of slaves who were sold out of Amelia to places such as North Carolina, Tennessee, Mississippi, and Alabama as the years went by. Later, by 1860, the slave population in Amelia decreased to 7,655. After being sold to their new slaveholders, many of the slaves out of Amelia were tragically separated from their parents, their children, and their spouses as they were forced to travel, on foot, to their new locations; in some cases, many of them never saw their loved ones again. Inside every plantation, the owner would put someone in the position of the "overseer" and in most cases the overseer was black. Their primary job was to oversee the function of the plantation and to carry out all duties in which the slave owner called, "Master" decreed. Overseers were trained to punish any slave that went against the slave owners wishes; for example, if slaves weren't working fast enough, the overseers would be required to whip them. However, not all slave owners beat their slaves; it is recorded that Rev. Park Berkeley, who was a member of the clergy at Grub Hill Church, did not believe in mistreating his slaves with cruel and unusual punishment. Unfortunately, the majority of his counterparts did not share the same sentiment. Slaves were beaten maliciously, by many slaveholders, they were whipped, maimed and a number were lynched. There were patrolmen called, "patty rollers" who were paid by the hour to catch and whip any slave who was found off of their plantation, at night, without a pass. Slaves weren't the only blacks who were under the microscope; many freedmen who were seen walking at night were killed or beaten by patty rollers just because of the color of their skin. There were some instances when a man or woman's freedman papers were torn into pieces by the patty rollers, and they were forced back into slavery. Even with extreme hardship and the pain of being separated from their families the one thing slavery did not take from the African American slaves were their songs. Because slaves were viewed as property, and non-human, they were many times underestimated. However, unbeknownst to their owners, many of the songs the slaves would sing while out in the fields were laced with instructions for plans to escape. Other songs were folklore to sooth

the minds and hearts of those bound to the rules of the land during the antebellum period. They would sing songs like *Jimmie Crack Corn, Deep River, Oh Freedom; Soon I will be done With the Troubles of this World, Roll Jordon Roll, John the Revelator, and Walk in Jerusalem just like John*, to name a few. Many of these songs listed were sung in chorus and response. The songs gave hope for freedom that thousands never lived to experience. They encouraged the hopeless, and while looking back at the lyrics to many of these songs, it's evident that they held the prophetic messages of the freedom that was sure to come to America.

Slave nurse holding white baby at the Wingo Estate in Amelia, Virginia

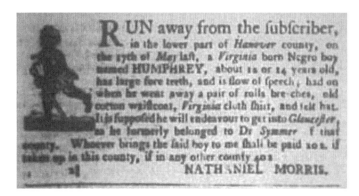

Red Lodge Plantation

The Red Lodge Plantation was originally owned by John and Elizabeth Eggleston Archer, in the late 1700s. Senator William Seger Archer, the son of John Archer, inherited his father's land after his death. He soon became a wealthy property and slave owner while in ownership of this inherited land. On this land, he later built what is considered one of the most magnificent mansions in Virginia, this mansion as well as the plantation was dubbed, "The Lodge." His sisters Ann and Martha J. Archer also lived in the mansion and owned slaves. They called this place home, and it was like no other, although it was unfinished, the parts of it that were complete were exquisite. It was there that Senator Archer and his sisters entertained guest while living what was considered a lavish lifestyle for that period. Until the release of my second book, "Red Lodge and Its Connections" there was little to no information about the slaves who worked on this plantation. Archer was so well off during this time that he also owned property in Mississippi; consequently, many of the men and women who were enslaved on the Red Lodge Plantation in Virginia were forced to walk to Mississippi all the way from Amelia County. After the abolishment of slavery, many of the individuals who were once forced to Mississippi decided to remain there to live as freed slaves; while others chose to return to Virginia with hopes of starting a new life there. Some of the surnames of the slaves who worked on the plantation during John Archer and Senator Archer's lifetime were: Archer, Hobson, Johnson, Banks, Brown, Thrower, Venable, Miles, Harris, Gray, Bolling, Jackson, Jones, Bates, Anderson, and Smith. It has been said, that Senator Archer gave a few of his slaves, each, 50 acres of land as wedding gifts but they were still bound to the property. The duties of these slaves were never-ending as they were made to work from sun up to sun down. Upon Senator Archer's death in 1855, his sisters and administrators kept the Red Lodge Plantation running, but their debts later began to add up. So, after slavery was abolished the estate administrators allowed the freed slaves to purchase their own piece of land, by making both verbal and written agreements, on the Red Lodge Tract. Although many of the former slaves bought a piece of land on the Red Lodge Tract others chose to move on to somewhere new. In the 1880's the administrators attempted to take back the tract of land on the plantation that had been legally purchased by former slaves. Due to this attempt a Chancery Case, spear-headed by my great-great grandmother Jennie Jones Hyde, was initiated in the early 1900s with Daniel Jones, Martha Brown Bannister and many of the children of the former slaves working together in the forefront of this injustice. In the end, the blacks who had since formed neighborhoods and a sense of community in the red lodge area prevailed and their case was won. Their portion of the land was saved. Today, Red Lodge Community, also known as Tyler's; Archer Creek Road, Rocky Branch Road and Lodge Court are still the homes to many of the descendants of slaves.

The ruins of Red Lodge before it was moved to Williamsburg, Virginia

Photo Courtesy of University of Virginia Photo Collections

Slaves and descendants of Red Lodge

Thacker Archer

Virginia "Jincy" Gray Archer

Jennie Jones Hyde

Royal Hyde and Rev. Daniel Jones

Martha Brown Bannister

Susan Epps Finney

Warner Banks

Frankey Miles

(1773 – 1865)

During her lifetime, Frankey Miles, a mulatto woman, was enslaved on the Oaks Plantation in Amelia, Virginia. This particular plantation was owned by Edmund Harrison and was located in the Mattoax section of Amelia. Edmund was a wealthy property owner who inherited a substantial portion of his father's property upon his death. This same property was also once owned by his grandfather, Benjamin Harrison. Not only was he a successful property owner, but Edmund served as a politician in 1801 and as the Speaker of the House in 1802. Frankey, who was one of his many slaves, was considered to be a beautiful young lady. Edmund Harrison's half-brother Nathaniel Harrison (who owned over 40 slaves and had roughly 2,536 acres of land) fell in love with Frankey. When Edmund found out about his brother's attraction to this woman, he conjured up a plan to sell her to a slaveholder that resided in the far southern states. By this time, Frankey had already given birth to two children who were fathered by Nathaniel Harrison. Their names were Laurania Harrison Anderson, born in 1802 and Edwin Harrison, who was born in 1804. It also is recorded that these two had another child, a girl, named Anna Maria Harrison Jackson, who wasn't born until 1820. When Nathaniel learned of his brother's plan to sell Frankey he devised a plan of his own. He convinced a third-party to purchase her so that he could, in return, buy her from him. The deal went through, and as planned this individual bought Frankey from Edmund Harrison; shortly after, Nathaniel purchased her from this third-party and immediately deeded her as well as their children their freedom on March 25, 1806. The deed was not entered into the deed book until April 24, 1806. Many slaveholders criticized Nathanial as the news began to spread both far and wide about his decision to be romantically involved with this African American woman. Yet, he proved his love for his common-law-wife by defying the rules and regulations of that period. Due to the laws of the land prohibiting the marriage between blacks and whites, during that time, the couple was never married. Nevertheless, Nathaniel and Frankey lived together until his death in 1852. However, even though the two of them had a close relationship, this did not prevent him from owning slaves of his own. According to the United States Census from the 1800s, Nathaniel Harrison owned 53-81 slaves between 1820 and 1840. His land extended from Truxillo in Amelia County all the way to the Prince Edward County line. After his passing in 1852, Nathanial's will was probated at the Amelia County Court; this was very upsetting to quite a few, especially to the members of his own family. The will of Nathaniel Harrison angered the whites of Amelia County; nonetheless, there were those in the court who honored his wishes and respected him enough to comply with his last will. In his will he left 1,100 acres of land to Frankey Miles; and this land extended from what was then called the Howlett Shop (near Five Forks Rd.) to Harrison Road all the way down to Nibbs Creek, near the Prince Edward County line. She became the legal owner of mostly all of the land that makes up Jetersville. To his eldest daughter he gave a certain amount of land, and to his youngest daughter, he bequeathed an amount of land as well as a house that, amazingly, still stands today. The records do not show that Nathaniel left his son any land or property; however, he did leave a sizeable amount of money to his four grandchildren. Frankey became the sole property owner of her common-law-husbands estate, and it is recorded (through documentation given by her grandson, also named Nathaniel), that during the Civil War, in 1862, she had approximately 19 slaves. These slaves cultivated roughly 2,000 acres of her vast estate. During those years, Frankey Miles lived a seemingly good life, but her way of living came to a halt in the later years of her life. In April 1865, days after the Civil War came to a close, Richmond was captured by union officers who began to invade plantations; burning homes, looting, and confiscating goods. Much of the crops and fields were destroyed as the Yankees made their way to Amelia; once they arrived, the estate belonging to Frankey Miles was also destroyed along the way. According to the testimonies, in the United States Southern Claims, of the witnesses to this tragedy the house that belonged to Frankey was unharmed, but the union soldiers stole all of her goods as well as livestock. Her grandson, Henry Harrison, stated that on April 7, 1865, a man named Phillip H. Sheridan and a group of union soldiers confiscated Frankey's horses, mules, and sheep; 1,200 pounds of fodder, wheat, and corn; other vegetables, 15,000 pounds of bacon, and approximately 20 pigs were taken from her property on that day. Frankey had become known as the largest black landowner in Virginia during that time. How devastating it must have been for her and her family to watch helplessly as all of these things were being stolen right from under them. Other plantation owners nearby such as William Anderson (Frankey's son-in-law), Alfred Anderson and James P. Anderson (both of mixed races) looked on as union soldiers invaded their property and destroyed their land and livestock as well. Not long after the invasion on her property Frankey Miles passed away. Once the dust settled, her daughters and her grandchildren rallied together and hired a lawyer to be compensated for the damages to the estate caused by the union soldiers. According to Mr. Lester Randall the home of Frankey Miles and Nathaniel Harrison was later sold, by the family, for $25,000 and the home was moved to Goochland, VA.

The descendants of Nathaniel Harrison and Franky Miles are countless and they are located across the globe. Many of the descendants still reside in Amelia; some of those descendants include the family of the late Pompey Wingo and the Anderson family within Jetersville, VA.

The former home of Nathaniel Harrison

The former home and land of NathanielHarrison

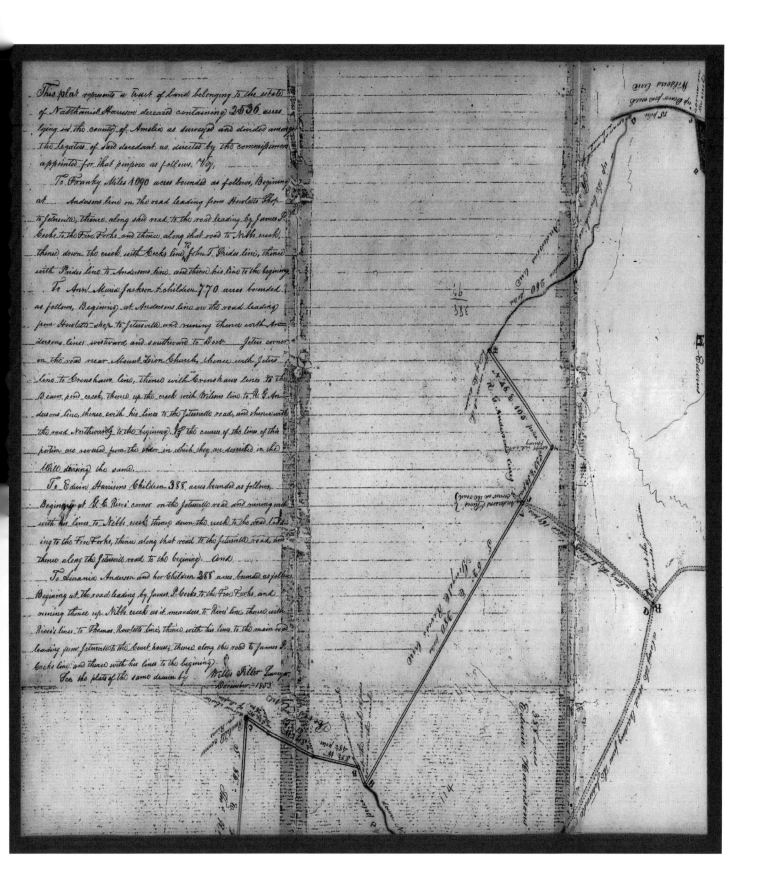

This plat represents a tract of land belonging to the estate of Nathaniel Harrison deceased containing 2536 acres lying in the county of Amelia as surveyed and divided among the legatees of said decedent as directed by the commissioners appointed for that purpose as follows. Viz,

To Franky Miles 1090 acres bounded as follows, Beginning at .... Andersons line on the road leading from Hewletts Shop to Jetersville, thence along said road to the road leading by James I. Cocks to the Five Forks and thence along that road to Nibbs creek, thence down the creek with Cocks line, John I. Prides line, thence with Prides line to Andersons line and thence his line to the beginning.

To Ann Maria Jackson & children 770 acres bounded as follows, Beginning at Andersons line on the road leading from Hewletts shop to Jetersville and running thence with Andersons lines westward and southward to Doct. .... Jeters corner on the road near Mount Zion Church, thence with Jeters line to Crenshaws line, thence with Crenshaws lines to the Beaver pond creek, thence up the creek with Wilsons line to N. G. Andersons lines, thence with his lines to the Jetersville road, and thence with the road Northwardly to the beginning. If the course of the lines of this portion are reversed from the order in which they are described in the well drawing the same.

To Edwin Harrisons Children 388 acres bounded as follows, Beginning at G. C. Rives corner on the Jetersville road and running with his lines to Nibbs creek, thence down the creek to the road leading to the Five Forks, thence along that road to the Jetersville road, and thence along the Jetersville road to the beginning. And

To Lucinda Anderson and her Children 388 acres bounded as follows, Beginning at the road leading by James I. Cocks to the Five Forks and running thence up Nibbs creek as it meanders to Rives line, thence with Rives lines to Thomas Rowletts line, thence with his line to the main road leading from Jetersville the Court house, thence along this road to James I. Cocks line and thence with his line to the beginning.

See the plat of the same drawn by Willis Jeter Survey December 1853.

Nancy Osborne Harrison: granddaughter of Frankey Miles

Mary Ellen Tyler: great-granddaughter of Nathaniel Harrison and Frankey Miles

Ethel Tyler Walker: great-great-granddaughter of Nathaniel Harrison and Frankey Miles

Anna Maria Harrison Jackson

On April 21, 2018, while researching the Amelia County Historical Society, I found a picture in a book entitled, "Old Homes and Buildings of Amelia County" written by Mary Armstrong Jefferson. According to this book, the house pictured below was first owned by Anna Maria Harrison Jackson. This house was given to her by her father, Nathaniel Harrison, before his death. I asked Mrs. Sylvia Gray, who is employed at the Historical Society if she knew where this house was located and I was pleased to learn that it was and could still be standing in the Truxillo area off of Mount Zion Road. As soon as I was informed that this house was so close, I requested the assistance of my colleague, Zavonda Vinson Parrish, who is a Truxillo resident, to accompany me on my search for this almost 200-year-old house. As we set out on our journey, we reached a street called Harrison Road which led us to believe that we were on the right track. While traveling back and forth on that road, Zavonda pointed to a white house and mentioned that a man by the name of Lester Randall lived there. This was not the first time I'd heard that name; over the years I've heard a lot about Mr. Randall, and I knew that I was related to him. I was also aware that he was an individual who knew a lot about the Truxillo area. We decided to stop by his home to see if he was willing and able to share any information with us that he could. Once I showed him the picture of this house he began to share with us all he knew about the history of it. I am thrilled to say that the home of Walter "Walker" Jackson and Anna Maria Harrison Jackson still stands today, in Amelia County. This is a home that dates back to before the Civil War, and I am honored, that the owners of this property allowed Zavonda and I to tour. Walking through this remarkably old house gave me a deeper appreciation for history. The realization that both a white plantation owner and the child of an ex-slave once resided in this house is mind-blowing. In her lifetime, Anna Maria Jackson was able to acquire approximately 2,000 acres of land. She and her family are truly unsung heroes of Amelia County. Thanks to Sylvia Gray and Lester Randall for sharing their immense knowledge and assisting when it came to locating this historic house.

Inside the home of Anna Maria Jackson

Emanuel Hyde III standing in front of the almost 200-year-old home of Anna Maria Jackson

Missouri Harrison: daughter of Lauraina
Harrison

Garnett B. Anderson: husband of
Missouri Harrison

Pocahontas Anderson

The Civil War

There were many Amelia County residents who served in the Colored Infantry during the Civil War. The majority of them were on the frontline during battle and some served as teamsters.

Here is a list of the Colored troops from Amelia County who served in the Civil War:

- Joseph Anderson (1843) enlisted into the 3rd U.S Colored Calvary on December 14, 1864
- Joe Brooks (1820) enlisted into the 3rd U.S Colored Calvary on February 24, 1864
- Steven Cox (1832) enlisted into the 3rd U.S colored Calvary on February 15, 1864
- Samuel Finney (1820) enlisted into the 6th Heavy Artillery on August 30, 1863
- Robert Gilliam (1835) enlisted into the 46th U.S Colored Infantry on May 1, 1863
- Bowling Green (1818) enlisted into the 46th U.S Colored Infantry on October 15, 1863
- Charles Green (1821) enlisted into the 8th U.S. Colored Heavy Artillery
- Magnes Henderson enlisted into the 23rd US Colored Infantry in 1864
- Richard Hendricks (1840) enlisted into the 55th Mass Colored Infantry on July 14, 1863
- Joe Hobbs (1810) enlisted into the 42nd U.S. Colored Infantry on May 29, 1864
- Edward Jefferson (1843) enlisted into the 5th U.S. Colored Infantry on December 1, 1863
- Benjamin Lewis enlisted into the 5th U.S. Colored Infantry in 1864
- Cornelius Lewis enlisted into the 5th U.S. Colored Infantry in 1864
- Charles Moden (1821) enlisted into the 37th U.S. Colored Infantry on September 26, 1864
- James Monroe (1827) enlisted into the U.S. Colored Calvary on September 26, 1864
- James Morgan enlisted into the 5th U.S. Colored Infantry in 1864
- Aaron Mumford (1844) enlisted into the 37th US Colored infantry on May 18, 1844
- Sidney Robinson (1843) enlisted into the 1st Colored Heavy Artillery
- Peter Ross (1826) enlisted into the 3rd U.S. Colored Calvary on February 15, 1864
- Douglass Smith enlisted into the 37th U.S. Colored Calvary on May 18, 1864
- James Thompkins enlisted into the 37th U.S. Colored Calvary on April 7, 1865
- Elam Washington enlisted into the 1st U.S. Colored Calvary on December 6, 1864
- William White enlisted into the 7th U.S. Colored Infantry in 1864
- Nathan Wilkins (1827) enlisted into the 37th U.S. Colored Calvary on May 18, 1864

In this picture, you can see a man named Tim Washington, who was a slave on the Jeter estate in Amelia Springs. The estate owner was Mrs. Peyton Jeter from Jetersville, VA. This drawing represents Robert E. Lee, on April 6, 1865, seen on his horse while Tim Washington is serving him his lunch on a tray. Coincidentally, this depiction was drawn three days before Lee surrendered in Appomattox, VA after General Grant and a group of Union officers defeated the Confederate Army. For years I wondered who this slave, Tim Washington, was and who his descendants are. I had no clue that I know many of them; some of which currently reside in Jetersville to this very day. Tim is the ancestor of the Washington's out of Jetersville, VA. I also discovered that several of Tim Washington's children are buried at the Holy Ghost Living Tabernacle, formerly known as St. James Baptist Church. Washington's primary responsibility on the Jeter plantation was to help farm the land; during his time as a slave, he was able to marry a woman by the name of Sallie (who lived from 1825-1927). Together Tim and Sallie had several children whose names and spouses were the following: Arena Washington who married Andrew Wilkinson, Marion Washington Ross (born in 1861) who married Abe Ross and James Irving Washington who married Callie Anderson. Their only son, James Irving Washington and his wife Callie, had several children as well whose names were: Pearl, Lewis, Betty, Randall, James, Sallie, Marshall Richard, Allen, Texas Washington (born in 1871), Puss Washington (born in 1873), Limey Washington (born in 1874), and lastly Callie Washington (born in 1878).

The Bells of Freedom

Bells rang at the end of the Civil War across all of Virginia which initiated the freeing of slaves within the state. Slaves from various plantations began to leave the land in which they had been enslaved on; while others chose to remain on their plantation because it was the only "home" they ever knew. The fact of the matter is slaves had no money or food, and so, for some, it made more sense to remain on their former owner's property; they essentially became slaves by another term—sharecroppers. The economic system was damaged on most of the plantations within Amelia after the invasion of the Union army destroyed a majority of their land and crops. Consequently, the Confederacy ended and a host of plantation owners struggled financially. Some former slaveholders, due to their financial situation, agreed to work for others for a dollar per month giving them the opportunity to hold on to some of their crops while living on the land. This was a huge turning point for everyone during this time. Other previous slaves found opportunities to work for small wages to earn enough to become landowners themselves; still, some saw no opportunities in Amelia and chose instead to head North for a better life.

Slavery by Another Name

After the ending of slavery, to control former slaves, Virginia passed an act called the Punishment of Vagrants which targeted the unemployed. This act stated that unemployed former slaves who had no income or who refused to gain employment would be arrested or hired out to work on plantations. Some freedmen refused to work because they were only being offered a $1.50 per month to work on plantations. Of course, previous slaveholders, who at that time began to be referred to as farm managers, found it difficult to maintain the functioning of their plantation without slave workers. Therefore, this law benefited plantation owners because it still kept blacks bound to the land and kept the production going.

On March 3, 1865, during President Lincoln's Administration, Congress passed the Freedman's Bureau Bill which assisted with providing aid to 4 million newly freed slaves. This aid helped them find new homes, employment, healthcare, and opportunities.

Carpet Baggers

Carpet Baggers were northerners who moved to the South after the Civil War. Many of them traveled while carrying their personal belongings in bags. Moving to the South they hoped to grow economically as they worked on behalf of newly freed slaves. The Carpet Baggers were known for shaping the new southern government.

Reconstructions for African Americans

From 1869 to 1890 Black America began to rise in power during the Reconstruction Period. This introduced opportunities for African Americans to voice their opinions and to take their place in society. During this time there were approximately 100 black representatives who were elected into the Virginia General Assembly. State laws were changed, and new regulations in regards to racial violence and the prohibition of whipping were passed. This outraged many whites in the South who were fighting to maintain the laws of the Confederacy. In response to these changes, white supremacy groups in the South began to torture as well as kill many of the Republicans and outspoken freedmen. Acts of terror were rampant across the South causing many blacks to become fearful; still, others continued to persevere in faith and stand up for what they believed in.

Samantha Jane Neil

(August 3, 1836 –November 17, 1909)

The Mother of African American Education in the South

Her full name was Samantha Jane Travis Neil, and this great woman was born on August 3, 1836, to Samuel and Matilda Travis in Clarion, Pennsylvania. She was reared in the Presbyterian faith and was trained as a teacher in the schools. On June 5, 1862, Samantha married a man by the name of Hugh S. Neil in Clarion, PA. Their marriage was short-lived; two months after the wedded, Hugh enlisted in the Company K No. 148 Pennsylvania Regiment, as a Union soldier, to fight in the Civil War. Unfortunately, he lost his life on May 2, 1863, in Amelia County, a week before Robert E. Lee surrendered in Appomattox, VA. After Samantha received the news of her ex-husband's death, she made arrangements to make the ten-day journey from Pennsylvania to Virginia. To get to Virginia, Mrs. Neil traveled by stagecoach, riverboat, and train. Once she arrived in the Big Oak area of Amelia she began searching for her husband's grave. There were countless hours spent sifting through the grave markers of fallen soldiers, but Hugh's burial site was never found. However, while in Big Oaks she met a number of newly freed slaves, and quickly realized that many of them were unlearned; it was then when Samantha received the God-given call to teach and demonstrate God's love for all mankind. So, on March 23, 1866, she began her work towards educating African Americans in Amelia, VA. She taught her first class under a big oak tree, teaching from her one and only book, her bible. News began to spread about, "the white lady who taught blacks" while the number of her pupils grew to

leaps and bounds. Samantha taught the young and old, as many began to travel from far distances to be under her tutelage. She also converted many to Christ and to the Presbyterian faith. Samantha was later permitted to use the old blacksmith shop that was beside the big oak tree as a school. According to the book, Home Mission Monthly, which was released in 1900, Samantha described the school room as having an earthen floor, a clapboard roof that was filled with holes and students who used logs as seats. Samantha taught there for three years and later used her $8.00 widow's pension, to have a log church erected nearby. She named this church Big Oak Presbyterian Church, and also used it as a schoolhouse. Mrs. Neil, with the assistance of other teachers, worked faithfully

at Big Oak. The school operated seven days a week from 9am until 5pm.days a week from 9am until 5pm.

On Saturdays she taught sewing class for women and on Sunday she held Sunday school teachings as well as Worship services. Samantha and other missionaries such as Rev. T. G. Murphy (a native of Dover, Delaware and a member of the Freedmen Committee) organized other churches. These churches were Albright, Russell Grove, Mt. Herman, Crewe, Jetersville and Oak Grove Presbyterian Church.

As her influence began to spread throughout the county and surrounding areas, other missionaries began to take hold of Mrs. Neil's vision and passion for educating African Americans. Around 1869 another school was erected, in Amelia Courthouse, called the Russell Grove School. This school was named after Mrs. N.C. Russell who opened the institution but was forced to return to Pennsylvania to care for her sick mother; Samantha took over the supervision of this school once Mrs. Russell left. There were dedicated teachers during that time, such as Mrs. Craig, who also assisted with teaching the Russell Grove students. She remained at Russell Grove until the pupils outgrew the school causing the classes to be moved to a brick structure in Burkeville, VA, which was named the Ingleside Seminary. Samantha's aim to teach the masses caused her to spread her schools to various communities within Amelia. She opened a school in an abandoned farmhouse in Jetersville, VA where nearly 100 pupils were taught. In 1887, with the help of her northern missionary friends, Samantha purchased a small lot in Jetersville to build a church and a home. Many helped her; neighbors and friends purchased the lumber while carpenters Robert Claiborne and Wilbur Hill, who were former students, constructed the buildings. The church that was built, which also was used as a place to teach students, was named Allen Memorial Presbyterian Church. It's evident that Samantha had a big heart as she opened her home to many of the youth who lost their parents—she acted as a mother to many of the students she taught. In 1900, Mrs. Neil was celebrated at Russell Grove for her dedication to the education of African Americans.

Many ministers such as Rev. William Henry Shepperson, and Rev. Charles Pitchford were very close friends of Mrs. Neil. She was well loved by people of all colors, religions, and faiths; and was even referred to by many as the "Saint of God." It was a sad day when Samantha Neil passed away, on November 17, 1909, in her home while surrounded by many friends, both black and white. People traveled long distances to pay their last respects to Samantha; at her funeral, Rev. Charles Percy Pitchford, Rev. Charles Booker, Rev. E.F Eggleston, and Rev. William Shepperson eulogized the woman who gave what little she had to create an everlasting impact on African American education. Mrs. Samantha Jane Neil was buried with many of the African American students she loved so well, at what is now known as the Neil Memorial Cemetery, which is located in Jetersville, VA on Drinkard Road. Some of the families who are buried in the Neil Memorial Cemetery are the Pitchford, Shepperson, Oulds, Delaney, and Booker families to name a few. In 1910, a monument was erected at her gravesite, and it still stands tall today in the memory of Mrs. Samantha Jane Neil.

Picture of Russell Grove Presbyterian Chapel

Mrs. S.J. Neil and her sister, Miss Tillie Travis at School.

Allen Memorial Presbyterian Church

At the grave site of Samantha Neil—a special thanks to Sylvia Gray, of the Amelia Historical Society, for always pointing me in the right direction.

The Honorable Rev. McDowell Delaney

(June 30, 1844 – May 31, 1926)

McDowell Delaney, a man who won despite the odds. This is a man who trudged forward doing things that many African Americans didn't have the opportunity to do or perhaps some didn't dare to attempt. He existed during an era in which African Americans were highly disregarded. Still, although the fog of racism and prejudice was thick, he didn't allow it to cloud his vision or stop him from accomplishing the goals he set his mind to. He chose instead to hurdle over the stumbling blocks that were bigotry and discrimination, and as a result, he became one of the most accomplished African Americans to come out of the county of Amelia.

This trailblazer was born in Amelia, Virginia in 1844 to freed parents Sarah Hughes Delaney and Edmund Delaney. It was unusual to hear of African Americans being freed in the early 1800s, but the Hughes and Delaney's in which McDowell descends from were given that gift of freedom. It was by God's grace that they were able to maintain that freedom as they were still living in a highly biased and racist era. McDowell's father, Edmund, worked as a miller and a bricklayer; he worked so diligently that by 1853, which was ten years before the Emancipation Proclamation, Edmund owned sixty-six acres of land. It is mind-blowing to know that a black man in the mid-1800s was able to acquire any land, especially sixty-six acres worth. I can imagine that McDowell's father understood the importance of owning his own land— when you recognize that your ancestors were taken from their birth land and stripped from everything they knew, you develop an appreciation and see the value in having your own. Surely, these same ideas and values were instilled into McDowell, by his father. Before McDowell Delaney's death in 1926, he succeeded in purchasing as well as owning his very own land in the county of Amelia.

By 1862, starting at the age of eighteen-years-old, McDowell was employed with the 14th Regiment Virginia Infantry; he initially worked as a cook and later took on the role of a teamster. He successfully maintained his position with the Virginia Infantry for a few years before moving into a different profession. It is documented that McDowell worked as the property manager for the Freedmen's Bureau Hospital in Farmville, Virginia, and he did this for approximately four years starting in 1865. It wasn't until later in his professional life that he began making strides in the political world. A world in which he never made any indication that he wanted to be a part of. It wasn't because he was active in Republican state conventions or African American mass meetings that caused McDowell to gain an interest in politics; instead, Delaney believed he had gained enough local prominence within the county to run for public office, and so he did. This was a monumental moment in history; not only was an African American running for office, but he was doing it in the first election in which African Americans were permitted to vote for the members of the General Assembly. On July 6, 1869, McDowell Delaney lost his bid for a seat in the House of Delegates, but this loss didn't stop him. In the following year he began another campaign for a position in the House of Delegates, and in November 1871 he won a seat as a Republican, representing Amelia County. Being the first African American to hold a public position was a huge advancement for the African American community. In that November election, he won with 965 votes out of the 1,367 ballots that were cast and defeated three other candidates who were in the running. After being elected, McDowell served for two years. In his time on the board, he introduced several pieces of legislation that he felt passionately about. He proposed several bills; one in which would change the state code in regards to offenses that were committed by African Americans, another that would require a license to carry certain weapons, and a resolution calling on the Committee for Courts of Justice to submit a bill that would repeal the laws that impose whipping as a punishment for crime. This man used the position and the influence that he had been given to make differences within his community and for the better treatment of African Americans.

After serving in the House of Delegates, McDowell moved on to accomplish many other feats. One of those feats was answering the call of becoming ordained as a Baptist minister and taking on the new title of Reverend McDowell Delaney. While serving in several churches within Amelia, he also organized the area Baptist Association that is still active today. He eventually became the husband to a woman named Mary P. Bolling, out of Cumberland County, and had four children. Towards the later part of his life, he moved his family to Cumberland where he continued to work as a blacksmith despite his age. After the death of his wife Mary, McDowell later married a woman by the name of Martha Mealey on December 8, 1903, in Cumberland, VA. He was the founding pastor of Chester Grove Baptist Church and served there faithfully for 35 years. He passed away on June 30, 1926, although his funeral was held at Chester Grove he was buried on family land in Amelia, Virginia.

We are so grateful to Otis Delaney, a grandson of Rev. McDowell, for paving the way to have his legacy remembered, acknowledged, and honored at Chester Grove Baptist church and consequently within the county of Amelia. Otis Delaney understood the importance of what this man did in his lifetime, and he we salute him for making efforts to ensure that McDowell would be remembered and honored.

During the time in which McDowell Delaney lived, it was unheard of for African Americans to be allowed the sort of opportunities that he was; nevertheless, being a free black man during that time didn't mean that things were automatically easy or fair for him. McDowell played the hand that he was dealt, and worked hard for everything that he achieved. It is evident that he held many professional titles in his life and none of which came without a fight. Apparently, he understood that anything worth having was worth fighting for.

Entry written by: Tanesha Delaney (McDowell Delaney's third great-granddaughter)

MONUMENT TO EXCELLENCE. Otis Delaney of Amelia stands beside the monument to his grandfather, McDowell Delaney, minister of Chester Grove Baptist Church for 35 years and member of the Virginia House of Delegates from 1871 to 1873.

Inquiring minds save legislator for prosperity

By Virginia McCown

In the dusty recesses of legislative history the significance of one man's career drifted slowly into obscurity. His name faded away — in part simply for not being included in a group photograph.

Although acknowledged as a member of the Virginia General Assembly from 1871 to 1873, the record that McDowell Delaney was one of the first black delegates in Virginia history disappeared from the State Capitol's legislative information. For whatever reason the chain of events occurred creating this error, McDowell Delaney of Amelia County, is once again being recognized as one of the pioneers on the road toward assuring public education, office holding and voting privileges for all Americans.

Little information is available

Delaney

about Delaney, and the facts surrounding his life are sketchy at best. Records indicate that he was born

See Delaney, page 9

Delaney

Continued from page 1

free in Amelia County in 1844. His father, Edmund, was a miller of Irish descent. His mother, Sally Hughes, was a free black.

Luther P. Jackson wrote in *Negro Officeholders in Virginia 1865 - 1895* that Delaney was taught by his father in the first public school for blacks in Amelia County. The year he started his education is unclear, but his grandson Otis E. Delaney of Amelia said he went to Chester Grove School in Paineville where he was taught masonry.

Delaney served briefly in the Civil War in the Confederate Army. Upon returning, Delaney joined the Republican Party, or Radical Party, as it was called then. During Reconstruction, he became a member of Virginia's House of Delegates. *Virginia Since 1861* states, "In the House of Delegates (November 1871) there were 97 Conservatives and 35 Republicans, 14 of the latter, colored." Delaney retired from office two years later.

Public records indicate Delaney returned to Amelia in 1873 and assumed the role of a coroner. There are also records indicating that in 1876 he was a constable. De-laney married Mary Philip Bolling of Lynchburg and had 11 children.

Amelia resident Viola Delaney remembers her great-uncle not as a legislator but as a minister at Chester Grove Baptist Church where he preached for 35 years. "I remember hearing him preach once but I was very small." She regretted she was too young to remember him well.

McDowell Delaney remarried and moved to Cumberland County. He had two children. Daughter Sallie D. Patton still lives today in East Orange, N.J. Delaney died in 1929 and is buried in the Amelia family plot. A monument in his memory was erected at Chester Grove Baptist Church where grandson Otis De-laney attends services.

For whatever reason the name McDowell Delaney slipped away, this week the State Legislative Information Department has re-entered his name as one of the first 14 black members to serve in the Virginia House of Delegates — along with the 13 other pioneers pictured in that old photograph in the State Capitol hallway.

Editor's note: This move by the State Legislative Information Department was sparked by an inquiry made by Virginia McCown.

Children of Rev. McDowell Delaney

Moses Delaney   Sallie Delaney Patton

Grandchildren of Rev. McDowell Delaney

Mary Delaney   Sidney Delaney   Otis Delaney   St. Clair Delaney

Grandsons of Rev. McDowell Delaney

Henry Johnson

(December 31, 1842 – February 7, 1927)

Henry was born in slavery, in Amelia County, to James and Louisa Johnson. He was fortunate to be taught how to read and write from a white male, who was considered to be underprivileged during that time, and in exchange for food, agreed to teach him everything he knew. His success with reading and writing put him in a position to become one of the early African American teachers in Amelia. He experienced even greater success in his life as time went on. In the year of 1879, Henry Johnson not only served as a constable in Amelia but he also, starting in May of that year, then again from 1891-1911, served six terms on the County Board of Supervisors. In 1889, he was selected to a seat in the House of Delegates representing both Amelia and Nottoway County. That same year, he was one of the 100-black-men who were bold enough to speak out against African Americans being denied the right to vote in Virginia. Johnson lived a full life, working diligently to help the progression of blacks during that time. He had the ability to purchase 105 acres of land in Amelia, where he resided until his death on February 7, 1922. He is buried in Jetersville, Virginia.

Edinboro Archer

(July 1849 – December 3, 1907)

Edinboro Archer, the son of a slave by the name of Amy Archer, was born in Amelia, Virginia; records show that his father was a white slaveholder named Robert P. Archer. While he lived, he also labored as a slave on the William Barksdale Plantation and was priced at $700. Once he was freed from slavery, by 1869, Edinboro moved to Richmond, VA and began working as a carpenter. After that he held several other titles; he was the owner of a wine and liquor store as well as a wheelwright, which was an individual who repaired wagon wheels. He married a woman whose name was Amanda Seay and by the 1880's lived on 1006 North Eighth Street in Richmond, where he lived until his death. Around this time, Edinboro joined the First African Baptist Church; however, he was expelled from that church in 1880, after he and four dozen members started protesting over the ministry of the Rev. James Holmes and Deacons. Later, by some, he was viewed as a prominent fixture within the community; and soon became the member of the Fifth Baptist Church. While serving at this church he was selected as one of the four delegates to be on the Council of Black Churches. This council assisted with the investigation of the First African Baptist Church in 1881. After serving on the Council of Black Churches; he was asked to sit on several other councils that included the Common Council which was a Richmond City Council Board from Jackson Ward (in 1882), and the Knights of Labor reform caucus, a council in Richmond City. In 1886, he was appointed to four committees of the Common Council out of Jackson Ward. In the years following, Edinboro had the opportunity to work as a foreman at Reliance Wagon Works (in the 1890s) and the Pioneer Transfer Company (in 1903); later returning to his work as a carpenter. Before his death, he even held a position as a superintendent for the Evergreen Cemetery (in 1906) within the city of Richmond. Edinboro Archer died on December 3, 1907, in Richmond, VA.

Robert Russa Moton

(August 26, 1867 – May 31, 1940)

Robert Russa Moton was born in Amelia County on August 26, 1867, to former slaves Booker and Emily Brown Moton. His birthplace was on the Hillsman Plantation, owned by Dr. Craddock. In the early part of his life, Robert's parents lived on two separate plantations; however, eventually, his father moved their family to the Pleasant Shade farm in Nottoway County where he resided. Mr. Samuel Vaughan owned pleasant Shade, and it was here that Robert's mother secretly taught him how to read and write. While on the farm Robert worked in the big house as a key holder and a house servant. At the age of eighteen, he moved to Surry County with the hopes of finding employment so that he could save money to obtain a higher education. Soon after moving, Robert was hired at the Hampton Normal and Agricultural Institute, where he worked in the labor yard. Eventually, he acquired enough money to become a student in that same institute and continued to work in the lumber yard by day so that he could take his classes in the evening. By 1885, he was admitted to the bar at the Hampton Normal and Agricultural Institute. Once he graduated he was hired as a teacher at an all-black school in Cumberland County, Virginia; while there he also worked as a farmer. In 1891, he returned to Hampton Normal and Agricultural Institute and was appointed by the school's founder, Samuel Armstrong, as commandant of the Male Student Cadet Corps, where he served for twenty-five years. Moton was held in high esteem at Hampton Normal and Agricultural Institute and was affectionately called, "major" by the many of his students. Robert was elected the President of the National Negro Business League, in 1900, and in that same year, he married Elizabeth Hunt. Unfortunately, they weren't married long, as she died just one year into their marriage. Later in his life, he operated as a Trustee of the Anna T. Jeanes Fund which provided financial support for black rural schools. He also took it upon himself to put together the Negro Organization Society of Virginia in 1912. During his lifetime, Robert had several mentors who helped him to become the leader that he was. One of his greatest mentors was a pioneer for black education as well as an author; this mentor was Booker T. Washington. Washington served as the first principal of the Tuskegee Institute, in Tuskegee, Alabama. For several years, Robert toured the south with Mr. Washington promoting black education and raising funds for black institutions. After the death of Booker T. Washington in 1915, Robert Moton became the second principal of the Tuskegee Institute. During World War I, Robert was called upon by President Woodrow Wilson, to travel to Europe to investigate the conditions of blacks in the area. In 1920, Robert wrote his first autobiography entitled, "Finding A Way Out"; which was a couple of years before he made another mark in history, on May 30, 1922, when he delivered

an address at the Lincoln Memorial dedication. Sadly, the racial prejudice during that time was still high, and because of this, he was not permitted to sit with other leaders who were on the program. In fact, throughout his lifetime he received numerous threats from the Ku Klux Klan and other hate groups as he worked to provide better education opportunities for blacks in America. His second book entitled, "What the Negro Thinks" was released in 1921. Overall, the influence that Robert has was national, and he became a trustee at many colleges in the United States. He eventually retired from the Tuskegee Institute, in 1935, after serving thirty-five years as principal. He returned to Virginia and lived in Capahosic, Gloucester County. Robert never forgot his family and friends in the Rice community of Amelia – Prince Edward County. According to his first book, "Finding A Way Out," he mentions visiting family and attending worship services with them at the Macedonia Baptist Church. In 1939, as he was advanced in age and nearing the end of his life he was honored by people of Prince Edward County; an African American school was named in his honor, Robert Russa Moton High School. Robert Russa Moton died on May 31, 1940, at his home in Capahosic, Gloucester County, VA. Today his house is a Virginia landmark, and the school is now the Robert R. Moton Museum.

Robert Moton

Jennie Booth Moton

Elizabeth Hunt Moton

Robert Moton giving the address at the Lincoln Memorial dedication on May 1922

My cousin, the late Grant Coleman served as a chauffeur on numerous occasions for Dr. Moton who is pictured six from left.

Robert R. Moton

THE death of Robert Russa Moton, May 31, removed from the race one of its elder statesmen. His was the difficult task of following in the footsteps of Booker T. Washington as principal of Tuskegee Institute, then and now, one of the world's famous schools. He carried on the Washington idea, consolidated the gains, and expanded both the plant and its curriculum.

It ought to be recognized that the presidency of a Negro college in such a place as Alabama is no bed of roses. A man has a tight fight between his conscience, his manhood, his responsibilities as a spokesman for his race, and the realities of the administration and continued growth of his school. Robert Moton resolved these clashes in his own way and it must be said that, all things considered, he did a great work. It has become known in these later years that several of the incidents for which he was excoriated at the moment were not of his making.

If any proof were needed of the creed in which the man, Moton, really believed, it is to be found in his astonishing book, "What the Negro Thinks." Here is a forthright statement which hardly could have been stronger had it been written by a resident of Montreal, rather than a citizen of Deepest Alabama. THE CRISIS joins the nation in mourning his death.

Above Photo: Robert Moton's obituary

Below Photo: Robert Moton's funeral procession

Rosa Dixon Bowser

(1855 – 1931)

Mrs. Rosa D. Bowser.

Rosa was the daughter of former slaves Henry and Augusta Hawkins Dixon. She was born on January 7, 1855, on the Clay Hill Plantation, which was owned by the Tabb family, in Amelia County. While Rosa's mother worked as a cook on the plantation, her father learned to read as well as write and worked as a very skilled cabinet maker. After the Civil War, the Dixon family was freed from slavery and moved out of Amelia to Richmond, Virginia in search of work and a better way of living.

Once in Richmond, The Dixon's joined the First African Baptist Church, and Rosa attended the Freedmen's Bureau School for recently freed slaves. Rosa was considered a scholar student, and after graduating from the Freedmen's School in 1873, she continued her education by studying Greek, Latin, and even music. It was around 1872 when she received her teaching certification from Richmond Colored Normal School and later began her career as a teacher. In fact, Rosa Dixon was the first African American teacher hired in Richmond, Virginia. While teaching, she met another educator by the name of James Bowser, who she later married on September 4, 1879. Together they had a son, Oswald Barrington Bowser, who worked diligently to become a physician.

Rosa's role in education didn't just stop at teaching. In 1887, she served as Chairwoman on the Hampton Negro Conference Committee on Domestic Science; and years following, in 1892, she served as President of the Virginia State Teacher's Association. Her lifetime work was not only involved in education, but also in civic duties; she spent much of her life fighting for women's rights. She served as an active member of the National Federation of Afro American Women as well as President of the Richmond's Women League. Dixon is also credited for founding the Virginia State Federation of Colored Women's Club, in 1908. She was a key player in several African American reform organizations, in groups that supported woman suffrage, with industrial schools for black children; and with associations that opposed lynching as well as segregation due to race.

Rosa continued to work meticulously as both an activist and a teacher until her retirement in 1923. To commemorate her lifetime achievements and her dedication to education within Richmond, the first branch of the Richmond Public Library for blacks was named in her honor, in 1925. Six years later, on February 7, 1931, Rosa passed away at her residence on 513 North Adams Street in Richmond, VA.

Rev. William Henry Shepperson

(December 13, 1862 – 1938)

Reverend William Shepperson was born a slave on the Shepperson Plantation in Charlotte County, Virginia. In his formative years he studied at the early Presbyterian schools; and, he later furthered his education by studying Divinity at Tuscaloosa Institute. However, he also had the opportunity to attend Biddle University Theological Seminary in Charlotte, NC where he graduated in 1887. Upon graduating, he moved to Chula, VA where he pastored for several years; later, he relocated to Ashland, VA to pastor a church in that area. Records show that Rev. William also pastored Oak Grove Presbyterian Church. William was married twice; his first wife was Zephyr Thompson, and from their union, they had three children. After Zephyr's death, William married Capitola Brown out of Portsmouth, VA and from this union seven children were born.

When Rev. Shepperson relocated to Amelia, he stood for many years as a pillar of that community. He is credited for working with Mrs. Samantha Neil (the mother of African American education in the South) at the Allen Memorial Presbyterian Church as well as for having ties with Russell Grove and the Ingleside Seminary in Burkeville, VA. He also worked for a period as a teacher and was revered throughout the county by blacks and whites. William died in 1938 and is buried at the Neil Memorial Cemetery along with Mrs. Neil and countless other students from the Presbyterian Church.

Rev. William Shepperson is an ancestor of many of the Pitchford, and Pegram families who reside in Amelia, VA.

Oak Grove Presbyterian Church in Amelia, VA

Estella Bradley Wingo

(February 22, 1878 – 1937)

Wingo was the daughter of William Bradley and Emma Williams and was born on February 22, 1878, in Amelia, VA. She primarily received her education in Amelia; however, for a short period, she attended classes in Pennsylvania. She matriculated to Ingleside Academy in Burkeville, VA where she eventually graduated in 1897. On June 19, 1901, Estella married a man by the name of Andrew Wingo and from that union two children were born: John W. Wingo and Donald Wingo. Her husband was the first black mail carrier in the village area of Amelia and perhaps the first black carrier in that county overall. Estella started her teaching career in Amelia, in 1897, where she taught for fourteen years. On September 1st in 1913, she became the first African American supervisor of the black schools within Amelia; and she held that title until her death. She was somewhat of an activist as she fought for the education and welfare of African American children in Amelia. With assistance from others, Estella was responsible for acquiring the brick that was used in the building of Russell Grove High School (an all-black school during that time). Her brother-in-law, Allie Wingo, sold six acres to the county in which the school was built on. Estella was known statewide as a, and a brief biography of her life is represented in the book, "Who's Who of the Colored Race" by Frank Lincoln Mather, written in 1915. I was able to speak with someone who remembers Estella Wingo, and that individual is Mrs. Evelyn Harris. She remembers Mrs. Wingo as the supervisor of the African American schools within the county. She spoke about how the students behaved a certain way when Mrs. Wingo arrived at the school—how they each ensured that everything was in its rightful place when she got there and that nothing was out of order. Mrs. Harris also recalls the little things about Estella's behavior such as how she would always carry a big bag with her. Mrs. Wingo died on August 18, 1939; her funeral was held at Russell Grove School and she was buried at Mt. Olive Baptist Church in the Chula area of Amelia. Estella has generations of descendants who have and will continue to do great things in Amelia as well as abroad. Some of her descendants were teachers; some served in the military and some are business owners. The African Americans of Amelia will always be indebted to Estella and others like her who, so long ago, paved the way for our education. May we never forget the sacrifices of Estella Bradley Wingo.

Rev. Charles Percy Pitchford

(1881)

Reverend Pitchford was born on April 7, 1881, in Jetersville, VA, and was the son of Charles and Alice Epps Pitchford. His father was a Baptist minister who was well known in Amelia and raised all of his children in a Christian home. In my research I learned that Rev. Pitchford is the great uncle of, an Amelia native, Chermine Tyler Booker; I also discovered that his maternal grandparents were John and Alice Epps, and his paternal grandmother's name was Mary Hyde. At an early age, Charles was one of the students of the great pioneer, Samantha Neil, at the Allen Memorial Presbyterian School.

Even when he was young Charles knew that God had a divine calling on his life and by the time he reached adolescence he had dedicated his life to ministry. Also, much like his father, Pitchford learned the blacksmith trade to earn an income. In addition, he also received a salary as a realtor and a mason for several years. Rev. Pitchford was presented with great opportunities in his lifetime, and some he seemingly wasn't even qualified for. Without a higher degree in education, Pitchford was still trusted to serve as principal over the Monroe School for one year. It wasn't until after his time as a principal that he furthered his education by earning an A.B. degree in 1904. Later, he enrolled in a theology school in which he graduated from in 1907. After his graduation, he became a prominent Pastor at Maxhaw Church where he preached for four years. He spent the rest of his life preaching at various churches throughout Charlotte, NC and was recognized within the community and best remembered for his sermons that he preached with power, conviction, and authority.

World War 1

Over 350, 000 Blacks served in segregated units during World War 1. Many of Amelia County black men served in the War.

Photo courtesy of the archives from the Library of Virginia

Union Branch Baptist Church

Union Branch Baptist Church played a significant role in the Civil Rights Movement in Amelia, VA; and it is a place where the NAACP held many meetings. It has been confirmed that in the 1940's the Ku Klux Klan burned a small cross on the door of this great church. This church is more than historical, but it has been a place of worship to many of the families within Amelia County; families such as the Randall, Patrick, Anderson, Tyler, McGhee, Wilkinson, Booker, Jackson, and Dickerson to name a few.

Liberty Baptist Church

Liberty Baptist Church was first formed by a group of freed slaves who were seeking a building to use as a church. In 1880, Deacons and Trustees Daniel Jones, Gus Jones, and David Scott learned of a building that was available to purchase after it had been abandoned; not only was that building being sold but the property in which it was situated on was as well. This building, before it became Liberty Baptist Church, was formerly another church called, Mt. Tabor. Coincidentally, Mt. Tabor was one of the many churches in Virginia during the Ante Bellum period. While in operation Mt. Tabor served as the house of worship for several families that lived within proximity to Genito Road. Some of the members who worshipped at Mt. Tabor were Rev. John Steger Hardaway, Edmund Harrison, Nathaniel Harrison, and the Featherston family— to name a few. All of the individuals mentioned above were well-known plantation owners during that era; the last pastor of Mt. Tabor was Rev. L. W. Moore.

With the shackles of slavery broken, the group of freedmen purchased old Mt. Tabor and named it Liberty Baptist Church in honor and celebration of their freedom. The first pastor of Liberty was Reverend Preston Smith; of course, that was years ago, since that time other pastors have lead this magnificent place of worship. Those pastors are Rev. Scott, Rev. Isaiah Henry Hines, Rev. Isaiah Wilkinson, Rev. Sadler, Rev. Manning, Rev. Neal Jackson, Rev. Robinson, and Rev. Kevin Jones who is the current shepherd over this church today. For 136 years, Liberty has stood the test of time while many of its founding officials and previous members were once slaves of the Lodge Plantation, Oaks Plantation, and several other plantations in the area. The deacons of the old church who served in the years past were: Henry Hill, Matt Tyler, Richard Dick Hardaway, Davis Brown, Wilson Tyler, Peter Johnson, Peter Clements, Robert Hyde, Joe Banks, Richard Watson, Walter Jones, Ned Ruffin, Preston Jones, David Smith, John Lewis, Joseph Bannister, Archer Jones, Roger Hicks, Arthur Hicks, Emmett Robinson and Freddie Smith.

Pictured above is the old Liberty Baptist Church building. In the early 1970's a new church was erected and the building pictured above was later dismantled. Pictured in the bottom left corner is the new Liberty Baptist Church.

Promise Land Baptist Church

For 138 years the Promise Land Baptist Church has stood the test of time. This church was founded in 1880 on the same land where it is located today. The first service was held by the first pastor, Reverend Thompson, outside under a brush arbor. The members later built a log cabin to worship in; until 1925 when the building that stands there today was complete. In recent years the church has been remodeled, and additions have been made it is still active today and can be found on Winterham Road in Amelia County. In the past, Amelia has been known for its great singing, especially within the church. One church, in particular, that was popular for its excellent singing was Promise Land. Mrs. Evelyn Harris, who is the eldest member of Liberty Baptist Church, remembers the singing and how she was always excited to visit Promise Land when she was a child. She recalls being able to hear the singing and foot stomping from outside the church; she also told of how a man named Sidney Epps would always be standing at the church doors when she arrived. The music was not the only element of Promise Land that drew people to church, but it was the profound preaching of Reverend Isaiah I. Wilkinson; his sermons were able to reach the hearts of the congregation. For many of years the Wade, Robinson, Archer, and Epps families were known for their musical talents in which they would use at Promise Land Baptist Church and within the community. Years ago the children of Sidney Epps and Correntha Epps formed a singing group; they were so incredible that when they'd sing at church, the entire place would catch on fire with the Spirit of God. Some of the early Epps family singers were Sidney Epps, Correntha Epps Owens, Deacon John Epps, George Epps, Mamie Epps Archer, Julia Epps Jefferson, and several others. Minister Larry Jefferson, the son of the late Julia Jefferson, says that his mother had a voice that reminded him of the great Mahalia Jackson. No other singers or church choirs in the area would sing like the individuals in Promise Land, and people would travel long distances to hear the melodious sounds of the great gospel singers. The services were always blessed; since its inception Homecomings at Promise Land were always a big event and revivals would usher in huge crowds. Brothers, Martin Owens and Rev. Chris Owens, explained how they remember when the windows of the church would open and those who did not go inside could still hear the sounds of harmony coming on the outside. In the 1960's Deacon Central Jefferson, another son of Mrs. Julia Jefferson not only speaks of the singing but the sounds of prayer that came from this church as well. He says that "people back in the day would shout, stomp and clap their hands giving praises to the Lord." That is the consensus from everyone who was familiar with Promise Land during that time.

Many groups and soloist have been formed out of Promise Land Baptist Church; one group, in particular, was the Inspirational Gospel Singers who used their talents for the Glory of God. The members were Correntha E. Owens and her children: Rev. Pinkie Royal, Min. Josephine Jackson, Rev. Chris Owens, Deacon Tony Owens, Rev. Lawrence Owens, and Martin Owens. Other members were Nancy Epps Archer, Virginia Scott, Marjorie Owens, Herbert Butler, and Mary Ann Epps Hansboro. Additional groups that were birthed from the members of Promise Land were The Heavenly Jewels, The New Testament Gospel Singers, and many others. Soloists who originate from Promise Land Baptist Church are Minister Larry Jefferson, Deacon Eyser Owens, Herbert Butler, Brenda Owens, and Gracie Henderson all of which are phenomenal singers in their own right. Even the youth of the church had the gift of song; so the Promise Land Youth Choir was developed by Deacon John Epps while Mrs. Daphne J. Holman served as the choir director in the 1990's. Daphne was a spectacular director and a great support system for all the youth. In the 90s the Promise Land Senior Choir with Mrs. Ophelia Epps, Mrs. Virginia Scott and several others would always keep the church in a state of praise. Many of the youth from Promise Land church joined in with many non-members to create a group called the Heavenly Voices. The Heavenly Voices were founded by John Holman, Richard Jefferson, and Deacon Sean Archer. The members of this group included myself (Emanuel Hyde III), Sean Archer, Travis Epps, John Holman, Aubrey "AJ' Mallory, Richard Jefferson, Cedric Jefferson, Min. Jason Holman, Jovan Holman, LaMark Butler, John Hill, Bernard Hill Jr., Herbert Butler Jr., Eric Owens, and many others. The Heavenly Voices were helped along the way by many people within the community. Prominent supporters of us during that time were Mrs. Mary Ann Archer who worked with the group by giving pointers and helping us to develop our voices; Deacon Eyser Owens Sr. who consistently cheered us on; Rev. Bernard Hill Sr., Deacon Central Jefferson and his wife Reverend Shirley Jefferson whose homes we used for rehearsals.

For me, one of the most memorable performances of the Heavenly Voices took place in 1996 at a program that was in honor of the late Deacon John Epps, who was a respected leader in the community and within the church. Although raised in Amelia he lived in New Jersey for several years in his lifetime; he married a woman by the name of Dora Archer Epps. Deacon Epps later moved back to Amelia, returned to Promise Land and served there until his passing. Unquestionably, he was a great singer and well known for his voice in Virginia as well as New Jersey. Promise Land was filled to capacity, and the program was filled with singers who were mainly from the Epps family. I can still remember the shouting and praises that went up that night. Mrs. Mary Archer sang, "I'll sing the wondrous story of Christ who died for me, sing it with the saints in Glory, gathered by the crystal sea." Min. Larry Jefferson sang a Sam Cooke classic and one of his own arrangements. Deacon Eyser Owens led "Sending up my Timber"; Mrs. Mary E. Hansboro tore the church up with her signature songs, "Send Me I'll Go" and "Walk around Heaven all Day." The Heavenly Voices performed three selections that night, the first was "Show me the way" led by Cedric Jefferson; "Send Me I'll Go" led by John Hill; and lastly "Silver and Gold" led by Min. Emanuel Hyde III and Cedric Jefferson. I even remember Rev. Lawrence Owens Jr. singing "Everybody Ought to Praise His Name" during the offering. There were other groups and soloist who took part in that unforgettable program. That evening was so electrifying that many people were catching the Spirit of God throughout the church. Without question that program will forever be etched in my mind. Even though time has passed and many of the older members are no longer here, Promise Land continues to lift up the name of Jesus through the word of God and the gift of song.

Past Members of Promise Land Baptist Church

Deacon Mason Archer was a dedicated member of Promise Land Baptist Church for a total of 74 years; and served there 60 years as a deacon. He worked as a farmer and retired from the Union Envelope Company. Deacon Archer remained active throughout his life; he even volunteered his time at the Amelia County Fair Committee, he was well known throughout the county.

Leroy Wade was dedicated to Promise Land Baptist Church and the community. Wade wore many hats and worked in several positions; he was Superintendent and Treasurer of the Sunday school. In addition to this, he was the Vice President and Treasurer of the Usher Board. Mr. Wade also served 26 years in the United States Army which he eventually retired from as a Staff Sgt. of the 300th SPT GP. He was married to a woman named Shirley Green. At the time of his passing, he was the secretary at the Obadiah Lodge No.170 where he also operated as the Past master and Treasurer.

Correntha Ann Epps Owens (November 20, 1930 – June 6, 2000) was the daughter of Sidney and Correntha Pleasants Epps. She was a devoted member of Promise Land Baptist Church. As mentioned earlier, she was a remarkable singer and left a musical legacy that her descendants carry on today. However, more importantly, she taught her children the word of God, and now they are teaching their children that same word. Her love for God, her family, and her church family lives on in all that knew her. She was the loving wife of Lawrence Owens; and their children are George White, Rev. Pinky Royal, Julia Wise, Rev. Christopher Owens Sr., Min. Lawrence Owens Jr., Minister Josephine Jackson, Deacon David "Tony" Owens Sr., and Martin Owens.

Virginia Scott (June 23, 1937 – July 18, 2017) she was a student at Promise Land School and Russell Grove School. She became a member of Promise Land Baptist Church at a young age and served there diligently for 71 years. At the age of thirteen, she joined the Senior Choir and remained a member of this church until her passing in 2017. Mrs. Scott was also one of the singers who were apart of the Inspirational Gospel Singers group. This woman was an excellent, anointed singer; she loved to sing praises to God, and she did it well. Her husband was the late Moses Scott, and together they had five children: Clara Chalkley, Moses Scott Jr., Clifton, Wilbert and Alphonso Scott.

This picture was taken nearly forty years ago. Captured in this photo are Min. Josephine Jackson, Florence "Cookie" Jenkins, Rev. Pinkie Royal, Deaconess Mary Archer, Deacon Central Jefferson, Rev. Larry Jefferson, and Rev. Lawrence Owens Jr. in Promise Land. It is said that the group in this picture was called the Heavenly Jewels. I can imagine Deacon Central Jefferson was singing "Hard Headed Jonah" or "Prodical Son" when this photo was taken. Still today Deacon Jefferson sings those songs under the anointing.

In this photo: Clifford Wilkinson, Stanley Wilkinson and Eyser "Ike" Owens Sr.

Mt. Olive Baptist Church

On February 1, 1877 Deacon Crockett Robinson, Ben Mitchell, Elam Booker, Henry Ross, Jenny Ross, Ann Murray and others were deeded a plot of land for the purpose of building a church. They were successful in building this church and it was named, Mt. Olive Baptist Church; since its birth, it has stood the test of time from generation to generation. There have been many who have received baptismal, taught the true word of God, and many souls that have been saved at this great church. Early family membership surnames were: Ross, Hill, Mitchell, Murray, Mondrey, Robinson, Booker, Baker, Archer, Royal, Epps, and Staples to name a few. Charles Jefferson, a Baker-Jefferson descendant, remembers visiting Mt. Olive Baptist with his family years ago. He told me the story of how people would travel long distances in order to attend the annual Homecoming Services which were referred to as the Big Meeting. In between the morning and evening services dinner would be prepared; some of the greatest cooks in the county would take on the responsibility of preparing each dish and the congregation would be served outside. Deacon Elwood Royal, who is a great leader at Mt. Olive, remembers seeing everyone's horses and wagons tied to the trees; he fondly tells of the old gospel songs that were sung by the seasoned members and visitors of the church. Every song would stir the hearts of everyone who was gathered around—it was a period when family and friends fellowshipped with one another and truly had a great time in the Lord.

Today, the church is still going strong under the leadership of Pastor Melvin Rose. Some of the current Ministers are Rev. Pinky Royal and Rev. Ervin Booker. Some of the current Deacons are: Deacon Elwood Royal Sr., Deacon Clarence Royal, Deacon James Archer, Deacon Eyser Owens, Deacon James Hill and others continue to lift up the name of Jesus. Mt. Olive Baptist Church is also known for their phenomenal singing; they have several choirs which are The Mt. Olive Male Chorus, Senior Choir, and the New Generations Choir, each have been a blessing to the body of Christ. Many of the founders of this church have several descendants that still attend and fellowship there today. The Archer, Oulds, Chappell, Staples, Hill, Robinson and Royal families have all remained faithful as parishioners to Mt. Olive Baptist Church and servants of the Lord. There are many great leaders in the church, and there have been several sons and daughters of the ministry who are now proclaiming the Gospel of Jesus Christ. The Minister of Music, Elwood Royal Jr., has served for many years allowing God to use his gifts to

reach people all around the county. His daughter, Shardae Royal, is exceptionally gifted as a drummer and uses her ability to glorify God as she plays throughout the community. Ms. Catherine Royal (a daughter of the late Mrs. Daisy Royal), the church secretary, the children and the descendants of Mr. Archer Royal have remained steadfast and unmovable when it comes to preserving the legacy of this mighty church. I commend them for always moving forward.

Some of the Founding Members of Mount Olive Baptist Church

Crockett Robinson was born the son of slaves on the Stringer Plantation in Amelia. In 1864 he was hired out to work on the Highway road fortifications. After slavery, he was deeded a part of the Stringer Tract and became a landowner in the county. Crockett had nine children one of them was Amos Robinson; and he had several great-grandchildren whose names are: Stanley Wilkinson, Phyllis Brown; the children of Clifford Wilkinson; the children of Herman Robinson; the children of Leon and Lucy Robinson and countless others. All of Crockett's descendants are too numerous to list. His descendants extend across the world. He also was one of the founders of Mt. Olive Baptist Church.

Paul Baker was born and raised in Amelia to John and Easter Baker and grew up to marry a woman by the name of Beverly "Belle" Branch who was the daughter of Peter and Lizzie Branch. His siblings were William, Silas (a twin of Paul) and Phillip Baker. Although he was a member of Mt. Olive Baptist Church he also fellowshipped at Promise Land from time to time. Paul and Beverly moved to Philadelphia where he worked for the Railroad. Eventually, they decided to relocate back to Amelia where they raised their children whose names are: Paige Howard Baker, Walter Baker, and Mrs. Elizabeth Baker Jefferson. There are too many descendants of Paul and Beverly to name, but a few of them are the children of Howard Baker, Rev. Pearl B. Carey, Lawrence Baker, Charles Jefferson, Monica Jackson, and James Baker.

Chula School

The Amelia Training School out of Chula, VA, was mainly a secondary institution for blacks that served grade levels 1-9. The principal of the training school was Lewis Green, and the teacher was Effie Scott. As time went on, the Amelia Training School was renamed Chula School. The renaming also came with some reorganization; a gentleman by the name of Christopher Columbus Archer was the one who helped organize Chula School, and also worked there as a teacher. Other educators at this school were Annie Wormeley, Clara Archer, Annie Johnson Booker and several others. Many of the children within the Chula community attended the Chula School. Several surnames of the students who participated are Mondrey, Harris, Robinson, Archer, Oulds, Royal, Hill, and Staples.

Annie Johnson Booker was the daughter of Willis Johnson and Jeannette Eggleston. She was reared in the Pleasant Grove Community where she attended Pleasant Grove Baptist Church. For a period, she lived in New Jersey where she became an educator. Annie married a man by the name of Charles Booker; after they were wedded, she moved with him to his family farm in Truxillo. Once she moved to the Truxillo area, she continued her career as an educator by teaching at Chula School. Annie Booker, after her move, became a member of Union Branch Baptist Church until her passing. She and her husband were the parents of Florence Booker Vinson who was the mother of Joey Vinson and the grandmother of ZaVonda Vinson Parrish.

Chris Archer, (bottom row far left) other faculty and patrons in the early 1900's.

Photos courtesy of University of Virginia Special Collections.

Brick Church School

It is not certain when Brick Church School was founded; however, this school's first location was a one-room building behind the Liberty Baptist Church. The late Mrs. Nolie Thompson often talked about the old school which she and many others attended. Most students during the early 1900s-1930s only made it to the third grade, and occasionally some made it to the sixth. Education was limited for African Americans during those times, and many were forced to quit school to work the fields and help their families. In 1931, a new school (with two rooms) was built by local carpenters, Royal Hyde and William Henry Green. Some of the teachers who taught at the new school were Alice Lewis, Mrs. Bettie Harris (who taught grades 1st-4th) and Mrs. Lucy Tyler who taught grades 5th-7th. Other teachers who taught at Brick Church School were Mrs. Geraldine Barley Scott, Mrs. Martin, Mrs. McGhee, Mrs. Blaylock, and Mrs. Stanley; substitute teachers during that time were Mrs. Susan C. Smith and Mr. Kemp Barley.

Many people within the community assisted with the upkeep and maintenance of these precious schools. For instance, in the winter months, Deacon Emmett Robinson and McKinley (Jake) Jasper would arrive at the school early in the morning to start a fire to bring warmth into the classrooms. A man by the name of Freddie Jasper would cut the grass at the school during the spring and summer months. From this school, many attended Russell Grove High School, and some students were fortunate enough to further their education by attending college. This school today is not in the best condition; however, it still stands as a reminder of where African Americans were once taught, and it is an example of how segregated the county of Amelia once was.

Brick Church School teachers and students in 1941   Carpenter Royal Hyde

Photo of Brick Church School students in the 1950s. Some identified, starting at the bottom left: William Hyde, Louis Hicks, Herbert Hicks, Archer Jones, Gerald Johnson, Welford Harris, Robert Robinson, John Robinson, Harold Banks and others.

Students of Oak Grove School in the 1940s

Lodore School

A Few of the Early Teachers of Amelia

Augusta B. Johnson (October 7, 1886 – April 19, 1982) was a teacher at Promise Land where she taught grades 1st-3rd. In addition to teaching there, she also worked as an educator at Chula School. Mrs. Johnson was married to a man named Lawrence E. Johnson and was an active member of Pleasant Grove Baptist Church.

Jessie Delease Johnson Hill (April 20, 1919 – September 1, 2010) attended Ingleside Seminary School. She understood the power of being educated so with that she decided to become an educator and taught at the Chula Elementary School. Later on, she transitioned in her career and worked at Russell Grove High School as a guidance counselor.

Dorothy Jasper Tyler (1904 – 1988) was the daughter of Thomas Jasper and Fannie Pride. Mrs. Tyler was the wife of Mr. Joseph "Moody" Tyler. She was employed at Promise Land County School where she taught grades 4th-7th. Mrs. Tyler was also an active member of Pleasant Grove Baptist Church.

Farmer's daughter led early reforms in black education

The daughter of an Amelia tobacco farmer, she learned something about farming, the planting, the fertilizing, and the harvest, a'like. Later in life she learned that people have to be tended to like the fields. If left alone, they too will grow wild and meaningless.

Retired county educator, Mrs. Rosa Martin, born in 1900, turned from the farm and applied the same natural methods she had acquired there to help educate thousands of black children in the county.

"When I started to school, there were no black public high schools in Virginia — only the first through the sixth or seventh grade," she said.

The education leader received her high school education at the Presbyterian operated Ingleside Seminary in Burkeville, a private school run by white northern teachers trying to advance education for black children in the area. The tuition for one year was about $40.

She never openly felt bitter about the situation that existed for black education here. Doing the most with the opportunity that you have was her philosophy then as it is now. But, then when it comes to a fighter, to get what you think you deserve, the best method she found through the years was by employing good common sense and also of discretion.

After finishing high school at that time, one could teach school on the elementary level. She did, for a few years and then went on to Agricultural and Technical College in Greensboro, N.C. where she received a degree in elementary education. After college, she taught elementary school to black children in Caswell County, N.C., before coming back to Virginia to teach in Amelia. She also taught for one year in Norfolk, but finally settled down in what would become her home and a 32 year vigil for education in Powhatan County, where she served as the elementary school supervisor for all its black elementary schools. Year after year the schools were consolidated, including beginning

in 1967, finally resulting in the one elementary school in the county, recently the subject of a countywide controversy.

"When I came here in 1935 there was a two room high school with one high school class and the other for grades 1-7. People who could afford to pay for their children's board and lodging in the community where the school was did so," she said. Mrs. Martin went from community to community throughout the county, spending her own time and money in an attempt to get children into the high school.

When she came to the county, many of the schools were in poor condition. "Pupils were drinking from a pail with one dipper. First things came first, and provisions were made where children were given glasses with their individual names on them," she said. "But, there were parents who even signed notes for money at the bank to improve the conditions of the schools. Five one and two-room schools were built with the help of the parents and the then white school board of Powhatan."

She rallied local black leaders to go out and purchase five second hand

Rosa Martin

buses to get the students to and from school. Each child paid 10 cents a day for a round trip ride.

"Yes, I guess you could say I helped to reform black education in the county, but I actually believe that after the movement for black education became stronger, then the state's intervention made it easier for me."

While Mrs. Martin was teaching and fighting to get better education needs met in the county, she took summers off to get her Masters degree in elementary education at Teachers College of Columbia University.

She likes to remember that there were many white citizens in the county who did everything they could to assist in her drive for black education. One very special person she remembers is Floyd Yates, who went with her to the school board and helped present her requests to the county.

When she retired in 1967, after working practically all her life, she wasn't about to oil the rocker. "If you've worked hard all your life, then you become a workaholic, right, not a sleepaholic."

She's never stopped trying to educate children, and opened up preschool classes or a kindergarten at her home for three years until the county system included it in the elementary school.

In 1970 she opened the Martin's Adult Home for the elderly, near the intersection of U.S. 60 and state route 522.

"I have six residents here with me and one full time worker, but I don't work quite as hard as I would like to," she said. "Understanding plays a great part in our lives. I just hope that I have given some of that to the residents of this community."

She wanted to thank the residents of Powhatan who helped make this last Christmas the best one her "folks at the home have seen for a long, long time." The list of gifts is almost endless she said, and will not be forgotten, adding, "kindness is the golden chain by which society is bound together."

Russell Grove High School

Russell Grove High School was first started, in September 1933, in an old historic chapel that was located on the Russell Grove Presbyterian Church property; today, on that same property, is now where Zion Hill Presbyterian Church stands. The teachers at Russell Grove High School were Mrs. Susie Shepperson, a native of Richmond, VA who was initially employed as a professor at Virginia State and decided to resign from her position there to teach at Russell Grove. Coincidentally, Mrs. Shepperson was the first teacher of Russell Grove. By 1934, only two instructors taught at this school; the additional teacher was Ms. Gertrude Bolar. Although there were great teachers present, in many cases there had to be special arrangements made for students to make it to class. Unfortunately, there wasn't any state provided transportation for African American students; therefore, many of the students were transported to school by teachers, volunteers in the area such as Rev. Robert Hyde (former pastor of Oak Grove Presbyterian Church), and parents who were blessed to have vehicles. Still, other students had no choice but to walk to Russell Grove each morning to receive the education that they were so desperate for. Eventually, a bus was acquired by Russell Grove to transport students to class, and according to my research, a woman by the name of Mrs. Lettie Robinson was the first bus driver for the school. Talk about constructing a new school for the African American students started to spread within the black community and works began to occur to make that happen. First, the elementary teachers, under the supervision of Mrs. Estelle Wingo, along with the county Wide League financed the purchasing of four acres of land from Mr. and Mrs. Allie Wingo; this particular land was deeded to the Amelia County School board. This same group also raised $2,500 to put towards the construction of the desired new school. Ultimately, a new school, made of brick, was built and within it were four classrooms, an auditorium, library, workshop and an office. The new school building was opened in 1935, and Mrs. Susie Shepperson was the principal; one year later, in 1936, Mr. William A. Brown became the second principal and served until 1940. The remaining serving principals were: Clarence C. Batts (3rd principal) who served from 1940-1941; J.A. Hubbard (4th principal) who was also a former teacher at Russell Grove; William Green (5th principal) serving from 1952-1959. Records show that the last serving principal of this school was Mr. Melvin Grimes, a native of Kilmarnock, VA. This man started at Russell Grove in 1951 teaching Vocational Agricultural until 1959. That same year, he was appointed principal of Russell Grove Combined Schools where he remained in position until 1969, when the schools of Amelia County were integrated. The first class from Russell Grove graduated in 1937. That graduating class consisted of Mr. Everett Banks, John Branch, Nannie Delaney, Channie Gray, Charles Harris, Conrad Harris, Marion Holmes, Anna Jeter, Graham Johnson Sr., Helen Johnson, Grace Jones, Olla McGhee, Elwood Richardson, Geneva Richardson, Sara Robinson, Elnora Ross, Alvin Scott, Henry Swann, Josephine Tyler, Virginia Watts, Blanche Ward, Irving Wright and William Swann.

Principals of Russell Grove

The First Principal
Miss Susie Shepperson
1933 - 1936

The Second Principal - Mr.
W. A. Brown 1936-1940

The Fourth Principal
Mr. J. A. Hubbard 1942-1952

The Fifth Principal
Mr. Wm. M. Green
1952-1959

The Last Principal
Mr. M. W. Grimes
1959-1969

Former school bus driver, 85, still active at county bus sh...

GOING UP — 85-year-old Nicholas Barley takes a ride on the handicapped elevator of Amelia County schools' newest bus. The short ride was "the highest I've been since the flight home from the army," he quipped.

He still drives a school bus every once in a while, even though he is 85. But he only drives empty buses to the shop for repairs or out on the road to rescue a disabled bus so the regular driver can get the students to school or to their homes.

Nicholas Barley began driving a school bus in Amelia County when "we first got a high school of our own" in 1934.

Mr. Barley said explains "the school" was the black Russell Grove High School, incorporated into the county school system when the schools were integrated in the 1960s, and he drove the school's first bus.

Mr. Barley made the run starting from his home in Morven, to Lodore, to Mattoax, then into Chula before heading for the school in Amelia Court House.

The 20-mile trip in the "homemade bus" which Mr. Barley helped build on a Ford truck body took about two hours while carrying 40 to 50 students.

Sometimes the dirt roads turned to mud and the trip took even longer. The bus might get stuck in the mud, then "some of the older boys would roll up their pants' legs and push us out," he said.

In 1939 Mr. Barley bought himself a new bus which he drove for 15 years, charging students $2 per month to ride. He did not always get paid, but he has no regrets.

He made extra money taking neighbors to church and the occasional church-sponsored trip. During Labor Day weekend in 1940, Mr. Barley drove his bus to the New York World's Fair on his longest trip.

The county began picking up the tab for student transportation in 1941, paying Mr. Barley a salary of $50 a month, but World War II interrupted his bus driving and he spent the next three and a half years in the army service serving in the South Pacific during the battles for Guadalcanal, Bougainville and Manila.

He remembers the fighting on Bougainville was severe enough that even behind the lines shrapnel went through the top of the tent where the ...

HOMEMADE BUS — Mr. Barley had his p... with the school bus he helped build on a ... chassis in 1934.

This newspaper article highlights the career of former bus driver, Mr. Nicholas Barley; creator of the first school bus, in 1934.

Highlights of Russell Grove

Russell Grove High School—completed in 1935

Russell Grove High School talent show

Mrs. Geneva Wiggins served as Supervisor 1961-1966. Then as Visiting Teacher 1966-1969.

The First Baseball Team 1938

Russell Grove High School: *Senior Class of 1938*

FRESHMAN CLASS--3 DIVISION

Class Officers

Banks Thompson--President   Frances Scott--Vice President
                Mabel Wilkerson--Secretary

Class Roll

William Fitzgerald   Virginia Foster
Edwin Hill   Alice Foster
Wilford Holmes   Gertrude Foster
Sylvester Jackson   Juanita Godley
Joseph Jeter   Elizabeth Jackson
Parmer Robinson   Maude Lewis
Lonadus Sesms   Louise Payne
Banks Thompson   Georgia Robinson
John West   Frances Scott
James White   Frances Thompson
Raymond Wilkerson   Harriette White
Bessie Branch   Mabel Wilkerson

Russell Grove High School: *The Voice* newsletter

The VOICE

"Flight to the New Horizons"

RUSSELL GROVE HIGH SCHOOL, AMELIA, VIRGINIA

M. W. GRIMES, Principal

A famous college president was being honored one night by a group of well-known educators.

"Permit me to congratulate you on the miracles you have performed at the college," said one educator. "Since you became president, this college has become a storehouse of knowledge."

"That is true," laughed the president, "But it scarcely deserves the credit for that. It is simply that the freshmen bring such and the seniors take away so little."

At this season of the year and this stage of your educational journey, congratulations are in order. We hope that we are congratulating persons who, unlike the seniors referred to

are taking away much more than they brought in as freshmen. To those persons whose years in school have been valuable, and by virtue of the fact that you are about to receive a diploma this includes all of you, I wish to express my congratulations and best wishes for continued success.

The test of how well you have done in school is just beginning. You will be tested every day and in many different ways. Your academic excellence will help you to meet and meet tests, but academic excellence must be accompanied by a display of morality, loyalty, sincerity, perseverance, ability, courtesy, benevolence, christianity, and tolerance.

Your parents, teachers, school, and community are expecting you to conduct yourselves at all times in a way that will reflect upon them. Your actions will be watched by others, and young children will imitate you. It is my hope your examples will be excellent ones.

As you travel the road of life working at your chosen labor task will be much easier, and your purpose meaningful if you keep the following in mind:

BARBARA THOMPSON, Editor

We present this paper with love and respect to you, our faculty and schoolmates, to give the future years a pleasant reminder of the never-to-be forgotten days of work, play, and fellowship spent amid the friendly atmosphere found at Russell Grove High School.

This 1964 edition of our class paper is attempting to preserve the personalities and experience of the past school years.

May this edition of THE VOICE help you to cherish in beautiful memory one year of the best years of your life.

— Barbara Thompson

THE GUIDANCE COUNSELOR SPEAKS

You are, no doubt, eagerly looking forward to commencement. As we approach the time, we hope that you are not looking at it from the standpoint of the end of your formal education. Graduation from high school should be considered the first big step in your preparation for life. It is our earnest hope that each of you will strive to continue your education at either the college or technical school level.

The age in which we are living is a highly technical one. In order for you to be able to make a worthwhile contribution to society, you must be prepared to offer as much as or more than the average citizen. I hope that you are not going to be satisfied until you have something of worth to offer.

I would like to suggest that you avail yourself of every possible opportunity for self improvement. It has been said by one writer that opportunity knocks early in the morning, and the reason so many people fail to hear it is because they sleep too late. Don't be among the number of late sleepers and allow opportunity to call and find you asleep. Nor should you be so busy in your back yard, looking for a four leaf clover that you fail to hear opportunity when it knocks at the front door. Let us not depend on the four leaf clover to bring us success. Success will generally come as the result of earnest and diligent endeavor on the part of an individual

Racism in the 1900s

In the early to mid-1900s, around the United States, racism was alive and well; because of this African Americans faced many adversities. Many of the added afflictions were caused by the rise of the Ku Klux Klan, a racist group formed in Pulaski, Tennessee, that spread throughout the country. This toxic and racist organization was responsible for unlawful beatings, lynchings, burning of homes, and the burning of churches. Not only were they responsible for these outlandish acts, this violence quickly became an ordinary unjust reality for African Americans of that time. There were a substantial number of lynchings, and murders in the U.S because of racism. Of course, African Americans didn't have rights during those years. Even when they were given an opportunity to be employed, they were usually overworked and underpaid. The ability for blacks to earn a sufficient income was so severe in the 1900s that many were forced to sell liquor in efforts to provide for their families.

 The spread of racism and segregation affected millions of blacks including those who lived in Amelia. In 1937, a Jewish educator by the name of Abel Meeropol wrote a poem entitled, "Strange Fruit" it later was recorded as a song by the great Billie "Lady Day" Holiday in 1939. This was a song that spoke out on the reality of racial injustice in America. The song opens up by giving the listener a full story of what the writer saw in the south. Some of the thought-provoking lyrics of this song are, "Southern trees bear strange fruit blood on the leaves and blood at the root. Black bodies swinging in the southern breeze. Strange fruit hanging from the poplar trees" it indeed paints a picture of the injustice and horrific treatment shown to African Americans in this country. This song brought awareness to the real conditions of the south for every individual with dark skin. It was a cry for help; northerners especially were outraged by what was going on in the south. This song also acted as a plea for others in authority to stand up for the millions of blacks that could not stand up for themselves. So much of the prejudice that African Americans endured in that period is something that many people today can't imagine; not only could they not drink from the same water fountains as whites but they were banned from using the same bathrooms as whites as well. I thank God that we don't live in that sort of era today; the kind of age in which blacks were prohibited from sitting in white-owned restaurants and if they did they were only allowed to eat at the lunch counters—in other restaurants blacks were only permitted to order their meal by going to the back door of that establishment. There were individuals in the 1900s who attempted to stand up for what was right, many blacks and some whites; however, because they were faced with constant threats, with some even being murdered, a lot of people chose just to keep quiet. Although I found no documented reports of lynching's taking place in Amelia during the 1900's, I have been told several stories by people from the generation who lived during that difficult time. Their stories paint a different picture. They state that many African American men were hung from a tree at the Amelia Courthouse for crimes they never committed. An older woman whom I had the opportunity to speak with explained to me how when she was a young girl she saw white women standing in the courthouse lawn to watch the lynching of black men. These murders were prevalent within the county, but no record was ever taken; in fact, several lynchings and murders occurred in the Painville area of Amelia, and the guilty individuals were never charged with the crime. This was the reality of how African Americans were treated not just in Amelia but nationwide. Let it be known that not all white citizens in the county of Amelia or the south were racist—there were those who supported African Americans and desired for blacks to have the same rights as the rest of the world.

The youth in the county did not have the opportunity to advance in their education because free education was not provided to them. From the 1920s to the 1930s families, communities, churches, and the use of song was the only way many remained encouraged and inspired to keep moving forward. The south was such a wretched environment for any person of color that many black families had no other choice but to relocate to the northern states to search for better careers and new opportunities. Unfortunately, not every black family could move up north for a variety of reasons, so they remained in their communities and endured hardships. Eventually, after a tremendous amount of hard work African Americans established themselves within their communities, schools, and churches. In almost every community in Amelia there were black-owned stores and other black-owned businesses including several funeral establishments.

The African American morticians of that time were John Lewis, Joe Bragg, Lewis R. Archer; Matt Tyler, who is the father of Frank Tyler Sr., and one of the individuals who owned his own funeral home; Vanderbilt Yates Scott, the original owner of V.Y. Scott Funeral Home, now operated by his grandson Reverend Paul Wilson. After speaking with many individuals about this time it is clear to me that black people worked together, supported one another, and shared whatever they had with each other. Maintaining a close bond with each other was of such importance to blacks that most of the black Baptist Churches in Amelia like Promise Land, Mt. Olive, Flower Hill, Pleasant Grove and Liberty held their services on different Sundays of the month. This method allowed unity to be developed and sustained within the surrounding neighborhoods. To help keep the black community informed there were halls built such as Lily of the Valley and Good Samaritan Hall, these buildings served as meeting places for African Americans to discuss issues or news within the community.

NAACP

National Association for the Advancement of Colored People

The NAACP organization was formed in 1933; however, the state of Virginia did not become involved nor did it recognize the Amelia NAACP as a county organization until 1935 – 1936. During that time, the president of the NAACP division in Amelia was Mr. Clarence Johnson, and Mr. Lester Randall served as vice president, in 1936. For them to gather together, they held their meetings at the homes of members, at churches (such as Union Branch Baptist Church), and at Russell Grove School. The NAACP, in 1936, worked along with the PTA, area churches, and other organizations to provide transportation for African American students for them to get to school. This organization was dedicated to making it easier for students to actually make it to school; in fact, Clarence Johnson, Lester Randall, and other NAACP members took it upon themselves to seek legal counsel in Richmond VA for their student's transportation. They were able to acquire a lawyer by the name of Oliver Hill, who was a great Civil Rights Champion. Hill was a Constitutional lawyer who teamed up with other lawyers and established a law firm called Hill, Martin, and Robinson, which was located at 623 North Third Street in Richmond, VA. Oliver Hill was making a phenomenal impact in civil rights cases throughout the area before members of the NAACP from Amelia approached him; therefore, they trusted in his abilities. The goal of Hill and the Amelia NAACP members was to obtain free transportation for African American students. I had the pleasure of speaking to Lester Randall, a man who was heavily involved in this matter in his early years, and he explained to me how he remembered attending several court proceedings and many meetings in efforts to win that case. At one particular meeting held at Russell Grove, V.Y. Scott, the local mortician, pulled his hearse next to the school and left an empty coffin there; to him, this coffin symbolized the time to end segregation once and for all. Many of the white Amelia citizens were shocked and outraged by this display. Shortly after that demonstration, Virginia passed a law which banned everyone from having public meetings at the school. When it was all said and done, the African Americans of Amelia County, being represented by Oliver Hill, won the case and transportation was provided for the students. Unfortunately, Oliver Hill was unable to practice law consistently throughout his life; this was because, in 1943, he was drafted into the United States Army as a private during World War II. For a man who was so accomplished in his life, no one would have guessed that he would've been called to war. Ultimately, Hill faced many trials while in the Army; he also experienced an intense amount of discrimination from white officers who served with him. The members of the NAACP also faced their share of discrimination, racism, and prejudice from whites who were opposed to the rights of African Americans. In speaking with Deacon Henry Foster and Mr. Lester Randall, I learned that both of them had burning crosses placed in their yards by a group of racist in the area. Mr. Charles Wingo, another man who lived during that time, explained how a cross was also burned in the front of Union Branch Baptist Church. Racism was so horrible during that time. One of the most outrageous incidents, shared with me by Deacon Foster, was a racist, with the intention of intimidating blacks, hung a black doll at the Amelia County Courthouse. Even with the hardships that they faced the NAACP remained steadfast and persevered. As time went on, the original President of the organization left Amelia, so in 1953, Lester Randall became the acting President of the NAACP while Deacon Robert Jackson served as Vice President. They worked diligently to obtain certain rights for African Americans; in my 2018 interview with Mr. Randall, he educated me on the fact that the NAACP and other pro-black organizations spoke on the topic of integrating the Amelia Public school for 15 years before any action was made. However, when it came down to doing it many parents of the African American children, due to fear, backed out of it which was understandable due to the racist climate they were living in. Several of the parents who were more willing to send their children to Amelia Schools were the Educators at Russell Grove; however, they feared their jobs could be taken if they rocked the boat too much with the desire to integrate the public schools. Still, someone had to make the first move; so in the mid – 1960s the first African American students walked into the public schools in Amelia. The first black students to integrate the school came from the Randall family, Mrs. Julia Coleman's family, Hilda Thompson and several others. Crystal Randall was one of the first black students to graduate from Amelia County High School in 1965. All of the students at Russell Grove School integrated the Amelia Public School system by 1970; consequently, Russell Grove School closed its doors forever.

Additional leaders within the community who have held a position in office with the NAACP: Deacon Henry Foster, Rev. Paul Wilson, Rev. Victor Livingston, Rev. Dorsey Drawhorn, Deacon Soloman Brown and Dr. Henry Featherston.

Mr. Vanderbilt Yates Scott

A titan in the African American community of Amelia, this man worked on many boards and organizations including the NAACP. He was one of many who stood out during the fight against segregation. Mr. Scott was a mortician and is the founder of V.Y. Scott funeral home, which is still in operation today. His grandson, Rev. Paul Wilson is now the operator of the V.Y. Scott funeral home; and is carrying on the legacy that his grandfather began years ago.

Voters League

The Voters League was a group of individuals who worked to have African Americans register for the ability to vote during the time in which Lester Randall served as Chairman and Patricia Booker Jones served as Secretary. When the league was first organized in 1947, they didn't have much success in signing African American citizens up to vote or convincing them to pay toll taxes. In fact, they were successful in adding only 100 black citizens to the list of registered voters; however, the minds of many blacks began to change in the 1950s and amazingly the league was able to register 1,000 citizens to vote in Amelia County as well as pay toll taxes. Needless to say, the Voters League was effective in making a significant difference in the lives of African Americans within Amelia.

Parent Teacher Association (PTA)

The African American Parent Teachers Association played a vital role in the school system during the days in which Russell Grove High School was in operation. African Americans attended the meetings that were held there within the community such as Lester Randall, The Richardson family, The Wingo family, Deacon Henry Foster and countless others who worked hard to provide for the students. The PTA consistently raised enough money to secure the Russell Grove School and to fund every event that was held there. Some of the greatest fundraising ideas came from this PTA.

Amelia County Civic League

This league was an interracial organization where blacks and whites worked together to better the county of Amelia. A man by the name of Lester Randall served many years as chairman of this dynamic group of individuals.

Rev. Darius Leander Swann

The son of John and Edith Elizabeth Swann, Darius, was born on November 20, 1929, in Amelia, VA. His father was employed as a farmer, and his mother was a housewife. Darius attended college and seminary at Johnson C. Smith University in Charlotte, NC where he graduated in 1948. Lee, as he was affectionately known as taught classes at Hanking University until the start of the Korean War in 1950. He was sent, by the Presbyterian Church, to China as a missionary and became the first African American Missionary to travel to a non-African country. He returned to Charlotte where he met and married Vera Poe in 1952. Once married, the couple traveled to India as missionaries where Lee taught college and Bible classes; the Swann's finally returned to the U.S. in 1964. When they came back to the U.S. Darius and his wife became the plaintiffs in the landmark Supreme Court case Swann vs. Charlotte-Mecklenburg Board of Education. This profound case shined a light on busing being used as a tool for desegregating the public schools. The case worked its way through the courts from 1965 to 1971; eventually, in a 9-0 decision, the Supreme Court ruled in their favor. This decision upheld an earlier Federal Court decision that ordered the desegregation of Charlotte, NC schools. This extraordinary case influenced much of the country, especially in the South, as the practice of using buses to desegregate schools became widespread. Rev. Swann appeared in Jet magazine on several occasions as well as in other black magazine publications. He achieved much in his lifetime; in fact, he wrote many books and plays, in addition to being the founder of the Maria Fearing Fund. From 1971 to 1984 he was a professor at Mason University; he also taught at Interdenominational Theological Center in Georgia. He has numerous awards and accreditations to his name.

Darius and Vera in India, 1952 photo courtesy: the Presbyterian Missions Magazine

Amelia County High School Sit-In of 1995

CLEMENT BRITT/TIMES-DISPATCH
"THESE ARE MY CLOTHES." Delmartri Womack says she will continue to wear ethnic outfits.

In February 1995, a Special Education teacher and cheerleading coach at Amelia County High School, Delmartri Womack decided to celebrate Black History Month by wearing African attire, which included a headdress, to school. On one particular day, a white student shouted at her, "Go back to Africa"; the response of the school officials was outrageous, they ordered Womack to no longer wear the headdress. According to the February 28, 1995 issue of the Richmond Times-Dispatch, former Superintendent Charles Shell stated that Mrs. Womack was asked to stop wearing the headdress because it violated school policy. The school policy stated that the headdresses that were appropriate to wear had to be related to religious custom. It was recorded that some of the white faculty and students had reportedly said that the headdress that Mrs. Womack wore was offensive. The ignorant and insensitive decision made by the school board caused students to rise up and take action. In response to the school board's decision, 100-black-students wore African attire to show support to Mrs. Womack. To add insult to injury school officials chose to postpone the Black History month program, at the high school, for various reasons during that same year. This just made tensions grow higher within the school and community. As expected, many students were outraged that not only was Womack forced not to wear her headdress but the celebration and acknowledgment of Black History month had been taken away.

Charilda Thompson-Harper, a tenth grade student in 1995, decided to take action; she could not understand why Mrs. Womack was told not to wear her African attire but when some white students wore Confederate flag t-shirts nothing was said to them—African Americans were offended by that, but school officials did nothing about it. With the help of her mother, Mrs. Hilda Thompson-Foster, Charilda planned a movement; she was quickly supported by her peers, Shareena Goodson and Sequoia Ross who eagerly connected to the plan, and together they organized the Sit-In of 1995. During that year there were roughly 502 students who were attending Amelia County High School, out of those only 183 students were African American. This story was reported to the Richmond Times Dispatch on February 28, 1995. It was that same day that the sit-in took place; 120 black students walked out of their classes at precisely 10 AM during the second period. Out of the 300 white students at ACHS, only 10 of them cared enough to join in the protest. This protest lasted for quite some time; ultimately these students did not return to their classes until near the end of their third period class. The purpose of this sit-in was to motivate administrators to hear what these protestors had to say. As the students sat in the hallway near the main office, news media and reporters began to gather around the school hoping to catch a glimpse of the sit-in that was taking place inside. Delmartri Womack told reporters, "These are my clothes;" and she was adamant that she would continue to wear ethnic outfits.

Student representatives Charilda Thompson, Sequoia Ross, Shareena Goodson, and others met with Dr. Henry Featherston who was at the time, the Director of Education Services. The students were well organized and came fully prepared with their six requests:

1) For the school to drop its rule of barring women from wearing headdresses.
2) Teaching more about the contributions of blacks & black history throughout the year.
3) To always hold the Black History Month program in February, annually.
4) For the school to enforce the rules within its handbook so that there is equality amongst all students.
5) To have the school arrange a meeting with the students and the Parent Teachers Association.
6) Lastly, they requested for the school to respond more actively to acts of prejudice.

This movement affected many students that year; in fact, a former 9th grade student by the name of Shante Meyers had just moved to Amelia, VA from Harlem, New York months before the protest occurred and stated that she remembers walking out of class and participating in the sit-in. She expressed how that moment made her feel like they were going back in time to the Civil Rights Movement. Having to go through that kind of experience was something students, parents and grandparents went through during the 1950s and 1960s but to face it in 1995 made her feel some kind of way. She furthered explained that it felt as if the segregation that was written about in her history books had resurrected itself. Tabitha Royal, who was also a student representative, spoke out against these injustices to the Richmond Times Dispatch. She announced that if changes were not made she and her peers were prepared to continue the sit-in seven days a week. Needless to say because of the efforts of Charilda Thompson, Tabitha Royal, Sequoia Ross, Shareena Goodson, Mrs. Delmartri Womack and many other students the policies of the school were changed. In March 1995 the school board finally allowed the Black History Month Program, which should have taken place the month prior, to be held. The ACHS Chorus sang High Places, Shante Meyers recited the famous poem Still I Rise (written by Dr. Maya Angelou), and guest speaker Delegate Riley Ingram of Hopewell addressed the assembly. Not only is Mrs. Womack an unsung hero for standing firm on what she knew was right but the students mentioned above for being bold, fearless, and steadfast in the things in which they believed in. Thank God for the Sit-In of 1995.

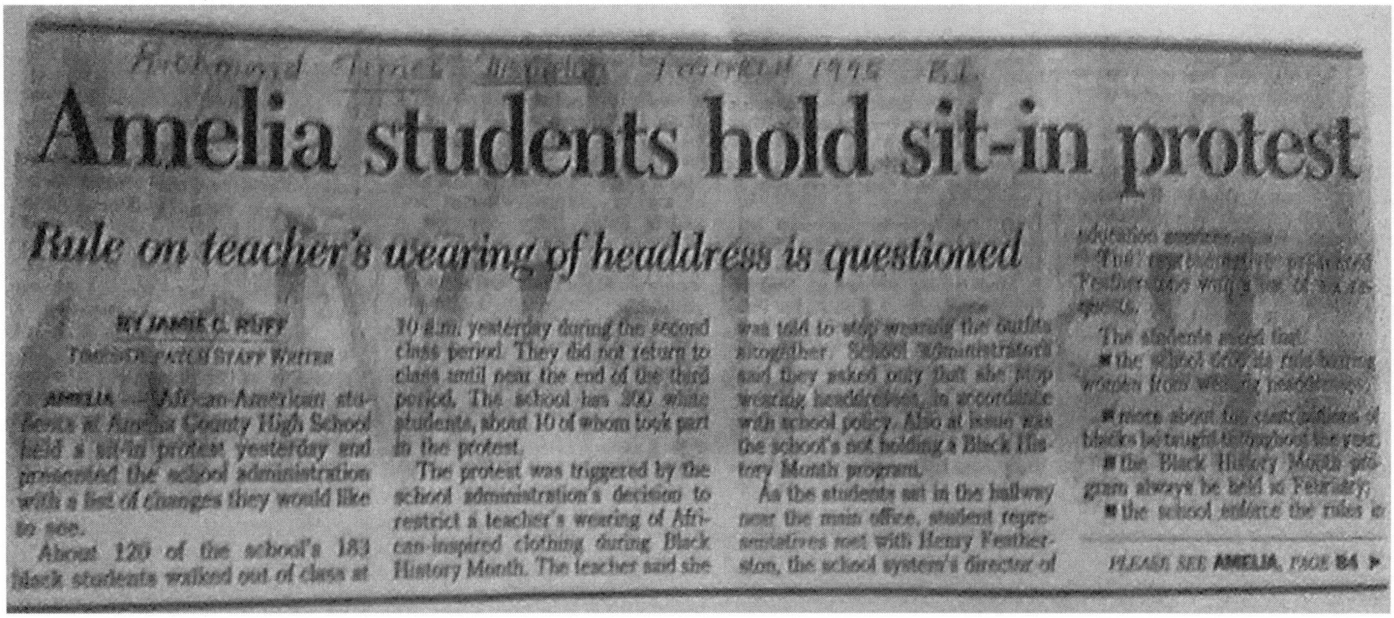

Amelia students hold sit-in protest

Rule on teacher's wearing of headdress is questioned

BY JAMIE C. RUFF
TIMES-DISPATCH STAFF WRITER

AMELIA — African-American students at Amelia County High School held a sit-in protest yesterday and presented the school administration with a list of changes they would like to see.

About 120 of the school's 183 black students walked out of class at 10 a.m. yesterday during the second class period. They did not return to class until near the end of the third period. The school has 300 white students, about 10 of whom took part in the protest.

The protest was triggered by the school administration's decision to restrict a teacher's wearing of African-inspired clothing during Black History Month. The teacher said she was told to stop wearing the outfits altogether. School administrators said they asked only that she stop wearing headdresses, in accordance with school policy. Also at issue was the school's not holding a Black History Month program.

As the students sat in the hallway near the main office, student representatives met with Henry Featherston, the school system's director of education [illegible].

The representatives presented Featherston with a list of requests.

The students asked that:

■ the school drop its rule barring women from wearing headdresses;

■ more about the contributions of blacks be taught throughout the year;

■ the Black History Month program always be held in February;

■ the school enforce the rules [illegible]

PLEASE SEE AMELIA, PAGE B4 ▶

The late Dr. Henry Featherston (pictured left) meets with student representatives during the sit-in.

Some of the Black owned Businesses, Games and Recreational Activities in Amelia

In almost every African American neighborhood in Amelia County, there were stores, hunting clubs, sports and recreational activities that one could take part in. People would travel to these neighborhoods to spend time with one another by partying, playing sports, or simply hanging out in the stores or clubs.

Polly's Play house

Polly Jackson Robinson out of the Lodore area was the owner of Polly's Playhouse which was a hangout spot at Lodore School once classes were dismissed for the day. Polly married a man by the name of Richard Robinson from the Pleasant Grove community; however, she became a widow after her husband was killed in World War II. Many people enjoyed hanging out at the Playhouse where they would drink and danced the night away.

Tyler's Store

Since the early 1900's the Tyler family has been known for their entrepreneurship and being early black store owners in the community of Red Lodge. Matt Tyler wasn't only the first store owner within the Tyler family, but he also was a mortician and the owner of Tyler's Funeral home. Tyler's home and store were located on his property on Archer's creek road beside the Hyde family land. Frank Tyler, the son of Matt, also owned a store in which he called F.B. Tyler Store; he built F.B. Tyler Store on his own property off of Genito Road. Much like his father he had a desire to own his own, and so in his lifetime he also became the proprietor of a funeral home and the owner of a baseball team known as the Amelia Cubs; their ball diamond was located directly behind his store. Mrs. Evelyn Harris remembers well the dances and various events that were held on his property as far back as the 1950's. For many generations, Frank Tyler's store and the Amelia Cubs baseball field was a main attraction in Amelia. Over the years some of the players from the Amelia cubs were Frankie Tyler, John Jones (who played on first base), Harold Jones, Clarence Randall (who served as umpire), Harold Banks, and Marvin Broadnax (who played on third base). The coaches of the team were Reuben Broadnax, and Henry Thomas Broadnax. Some of the players of the team were Junius Smith, Sylvester Robinson and some of his brothers also Robert Barley and others. During many of the games, and a gentleman by the name of Solomon Banks served as the DJ and announcer. The baseball games in Amelia didn't only attract people from within that county, but visitors would travel from Goochland, Cumberland, Richmond, and beyond to be spectators of the game. There are people within this county who remember those days very well; for example, Mrs. Vera Gibson, a long time resident of Amelia shared with me her memory of attending the games at Tyler's every Saturday, she and her sisters, to watch their brothers play ball. There was a great camaraderie amongst the team members and desire to be the best; Mr. Tyler would often tell his teams if any one of them hit the ball out the park he would give them twenty dollars. After the passing of Mr. Tyler, his son Frank Tyler Jr. began to operate the store, and did so for a long period of time; he also became the owner of the Amelia Cubs and eventually formed a softball team. Darlene Lewis Robinson remembers the fantastic food, contest, and dances that would take place at the store. When it came to writing the history of Tyler's Store I came across so many people who held fond memories of that unique place. Another story that stood out to me came from a woman by the name of Rosetta Broadnax. While laughing, she told me of how one Saturday in the 1980's, while at the Amelia Cubs game, she was hungry and so she decided to buy a chicken sandwich. Rosetta said that the sandwich was so good that she just had to take her false tooth out because it was causing her to have trouble chewing her food. She explains how she was so focused on eating that chicken sandwich that she accidentally threw her tooth on the ground. At some point, she realized that her tooth was missing and she assumed that she must have lost it out on the field. Yet, the story doesn't end there, the next day she recruited a man by the name of Joey Vinson, and her sister Virginia to help her find her missing tooth. So they all piled into Joey's blue and white car and went on their way; when they reached the store, she walked to the field and by retracing her tracks from the previous day she was able to find her tooth. Her troubles didn't end there; at close examination of the tooth, she noticed that it had dog bite marks all over it. She showed Jenny (her sister) and Joey the tooth and said a dog tried to eat it; she refused to let that tooth go to waste, she took it home and soaked it in hot water and bleach. Once it dried she put it back in her mouth; Joey and Jenny laughed until they cried. While sharing memories, Rosetta also reflected on the dust dances that were held on the baseball field of those years ago. People would wear white tennis shoes to the dances and because of the dust and dirt, they would be orange shoes by the time everyone left. Back in those days partying hard was an understatement.

Buggs Place was located in the Promise Land area of Amelia and served as a social hang out spot for blacks in the county.

Paradise Hall was owned by Howard Epps. The hall was opened to act as a night time hangout spot for the night owls within Amelia. It first opened in the 1950's, and remained a popular place to gather until its closing. Howard had his own band that played there for years.

Frank Epps Store- Mr. Epps was a successful businessman who, years ago, owned the Frank Epps Store. Frank's store was known for hosting baseball games, parties and for serving delicious food. Many people say that they cooked the best fried chicken in town; they also sold chitterling dinners, fish, and a variety of other dishes. Frank organized several baseball teams for the community one was called Epps A, and the other team was known as the Astros. One of the coaches for his team was Mr. Pompey Wingo; and there were many team players such as Deacon Eyser Owens, Percell Owens, Deacon Tony Owens and others.

James Archer's Place was another store in the Chula area of Amelia. Owners were Mr. James and Victoria R. Archer

William Tyler's Store was located in the Red Lodge Community. This store drew many customers because of the pool table, and the pinball machine that was inside.

Elwood Royal's Service Station - Deacon Elwood Royal owned a service station in Chula called *Chula Gulf*. Deacon Royal successfully owned the store for five years; it was located exactly where the Exxon is now on the corner of RT. 604 and 360.

Louise Robinson Archer (store) - was a successful business woman and was the owner of a store was located on Rt. 604 in the Chula community.

Granderson Robinson Store - Granderson Robinson owned and operated a store in the Promise Land community. The late Granderson and his wife Nannie Robinson proved themselves to be great entrepreneurs. After Granderson's death, his wife began to take care of the day to day operations of the store; her son Roosevelt and his wife Dorothy also pitched in to run it as well. Mrs. Dorothy would cook bologna burgers and other favorite food items that customers enjoyed. Today, many of their family members still reside in Promise Land.

Enterprise Club—After the closing of Chula school its building was remodeled as a club called the Enterprise Club. A couple of the members were: William Tyler, and Westmoreland Thompson. The parties at the club use to bring a large crowd of patrons.

Disc Jockeys- the popular disc jockeys that would be hired to play at many of the businesses mentioned above were: Black Barron, Sam the beast from the East, Kirby Carmichael, The Brother Kings and others.

Picture extracted from a news paper article of Deacon Elwood Royal Sr. grand opening of Chula Gulf.

During the late 1960s and early 1970's Harold Jones organized a female softball team in which he named *The Red Lodge Pacers*. This team traveled to many surrounding counties, and they were so awesome that they made a name for themselves every where they went. Some of the alumni of this team are: Brenda Jasper Scott, Debbie Henderson Clarke, Anita Jasper Royal, Jackie Henderson Gray, Rosetta Broadnax, Andrea Banks, Sherry Banks, Brenda Trent Smith, Daphne Jasper Holman, Vanessa Yates, Karen Banks Carter, Rev. Rozena Jones Jackson, Gail Banks, Gloria Lewis Nelms, Charlene Lewis Yates, Diane Moseley, Shirdine Banks Harris, and Wanda Banks Spurlock just to name a few.

Rev. Isaiah Immanuel Wilkinson

(1886 – 1949)

A leader of his time

A voice crying out in the wilderness prepare ye the way of the Lord.

Rev. Isaiah Wilkinson was the son of Armstead and Cornelia Granger Wilkinson. He was born and raised in the Truxillo area of Amelia County, and he frequently attended Union Branch Baptist Church. It was in 1911 when Isaiah married the love of his life, a young woman named Lavinia Johnson; once married, the couple

 relocated to Richmond, Va. Isaiah worked as a construction worker and specialized in cement mixing to provide for his family. It wasn't long before Mr. Wilkinson felt the call of God upon his life and began taking night classes at Virginia Union University to help prepare him to preach the gospel. Once he completed his courses, he and his family returned to Amelia and due to his diligence and dedication he soon became known as a well-beloved pastor. In his lifetime this man served as pastor over several churches, and those are Second Baptist Church, which was formed out of Union Branch Baptist Church; Little Union Baptist Church; Liberty Baptist Church; Promise Land Baptist Church; Center Union Baptist Church, and lastly Good Hope Baptist Church. He was considered to be one of the greatest leaders of his time; he was a huge supporter and promoter of the notion that African Americans must be appropriately educated. Whatever Mr. Wilkinson could do to lend a hand to black schools or communities

he would. In fact, for many years, Rev. Wilkinson went out of his way to provide the wood that was used to heat Russell Grove Elementary School. He served faithfully on several boards and organizations including the PTA, NAACP and as the Vice Moderator of the Amelia—Nottoway and Dinwiddie Baptist Association. After the death of his wife Lavinia, he later married a woman by the name of Maude Evans Brown; throughout the remainder of his life, he remained steadfast to God and his calling until his death in 1949. Without question, this man left behind a legacy of faith and determination.

Rev. Isaiah Wilkinson baptizing a candidate at the Liberty Baptist Church baptizing pond in 1912. Rev. Isaiah Wilkinson pictured with his second wife, Maude.

The Wilkinsons'

Armstead Wilkinson was the son of Shirley Wilkinson and Mary Booker. He married a woman by the name of Cornelia Granger; they raised two children: Rev.Isaiah Wilkinson, Matilda Wilkinson Randall. (abt. 1855 – September 15, 1949)

Rev. William Wilkinson is the son of Rev. Isaiah Wilkinson and <rs. Lavinia Johnson Wilkinson. He was the former Associate Pastor of Union Branch Baptist Church. He served on many organizations while he was alive, and in his spare time he dabbled in basket weaving which he had a great talent for. Rev. Wilkinson was the husband of Muriel Robinson Wilkinson and the father of Phyllis Wilkinson Brown, Stanley Wilkinson, and Clifford Wilkinson (who was the husband of one of the great leaders in education Mrs. Catherine McQueen Wilkinson).

Fannie Wilkinson Fitzgerald

(July 27, 1930 – April 7, 2016)

A Civil Rights Icon

The name Fannie Wilkinson Fitzgerald has been permanently etched in Virginia's history as she was one of the Courageous Four during the Civil Rights Movement. Born and raised in Amelia County she was the youngest of eleven children; her parents were Rev. Isaiah and Lavenia Wilkinson. She graduated from Russell Grove High School and later went on to further her education by studying at Virginia Union University. Mrs. Fitzgerald desired to explore her education, and so she did, as a result of her hard work and diligence, she earned her Bachelor of Arts degree in Elementary Education. She started her legendary teaching career in a two room school house that was located in Amelia. In 1955, she relocated in hopes of finding better career opportunities. As time went on Mrs. Fitzgerald had the desire to further her education again and did so by attending Columbia University in New York City; this time she earned her Master's Degree in Special Education, graduating in 1960. Before her Master's program was even complete she began to receive job offers for positions that they wanted her to fill after graduating. Mrs. Fitzgerald received an offer to teach at Antioch-Mcrae Elementary School in Prince William County, VA. However, after her graduation Fannie chose to take a teaching position at an all-black school called Jennie Dean School in Manassas, Virginia; it wasn't until later that she transitioned over to teach at Antioch-Mcrae Elementary School. Then she was transferred to teach at an all-white school known as Fred Lynn Elementary and Middle School along with three other black teachers whose names were: Mary G. Porter, Maxine Coleman, and Zella Brown. Mrs. Fitzgerald and these three teachers were the first African American educators in Prince William County to integrate an all-white school; therefore, they were dubbed, "The Courageous Four." With their bravery, persistence, and labor the Prince William County Schools were fully integrated by September 1965. Well accomplished, Mrs. Fitzgerald became the first African American teacher to educate at Manassas Park Elementary school. Later, she also became the first elementary school supervisor within the integrated public schools in Prince William County. Throughout her career, she served as a learning disabilities specialist who taught fourth-grade students. Mrs. Fitzgerald was so excellent in her position that she was later promoted and became the overseer of all disability programs in Prince William Public Schools. After a satisfying career, she retired in 1988 but continued to volunteer her time, skills and wisdom as a community leader in Prince William County. In addition to appearing in several newspaper articles and magazines, she received many honors during her lifetime for her dedication to educating the youth. In a 2003 interview, Mrs. Fitzgerald reflected on her experiences during the desegregation period; within that same interview she was recorded as saying, "Those first years of integration were not easy for me, but I knew it was something I had to do." In the fall of 2008, The Fannie W. Fitzgerald Elementary School, which is located on Benita Fitzgerald drive, a street named after her daughter who is a 1984 Olympic Gold Medalist was built in her honor. Fannie Wilkinson Fitzgerald passed away on April 7, 2016, and she was laid to rest beside her husband, Rodger P. Fitzgerald, at Quantico National Cemetery.

Fannie Peyton Johnson Finney

(May 4, 1877 – July 5, 1950)

Mrs. Finney was born on May 4, 1877, in Amelia, VA and was the daughter of Willis Johnson and Jeanette Eggleston. While she was alive, she was a devoted member of Pleasant Grove Baptist Church. After receiving her early education, Fannie attended Ingleside Seminary. She did college work at St. Paul School in Lawrenceville, VA (years later that school was renamed St. Paul College); in addition to that she also enrolled in courses at Hampton Institute and Virginia State University. Once she was ready, she began teaching in Amelia, Powhatan County, Union Branch church, Belona, and Pine Hill Elementary School. This dedicated teacher married Mr. John Finney, who was born in Amelia County; from this union, they had thirteen children. Their children's names are Clifford, John, Annie, Junius, Constancia, Albert, Margaret, Jeanette, Essex, Emory, Novella, Paul, and Lillian. The couple and their children lived on the land that her husband owned in Powhatan, VA. It was in Powhatan that Mrs. Finney began educating students at Pine Hill Elementary School which was an all-black school; she taught grade 1st-6th. Although she was passionate about teaching, she was involved in other activities as well. This great woman served as a massive supporter of Pine Hill Baptist Church, as President of the James River Sunday School Convention, for many years; and also was acting President of the Powhatan County Teachers Association for a number of years before her passing.

John Finney

(1870 – 1951)

John was born in the Mattoax section of Amelia County to a woman named Susan Epps Finney; his mother was a former slave of William Segar Archer and worked on the Red Lodge Plantation. During her enslavement, she was also forced to work on the Fighting Creek Plantation in Powhatan County. John Finney's father, Essex Finney, was a former slave as well and was forced to work on the Mill Quarter Plantation also in Powhatan, VA. Mr. Finney was raised in both Amelia and Powhatan; once he became a young man he married and woman by the name of Fannie Peyton Johnson. This man was considered very intelligent in his time; he worked hard as a farmer and eventually was able to own his own land that was also located in Powhatan. Although he spent much of his time in Powhatan County he had a heart for Amelia—he was a member of Liberty Baptist Church (in Amelia) and is buried at Pleasant Grove Baptist Church.

Rev. Horace Montague

(October 4, 1921 – May 28, 1994)

The Shout Preserver

"God built the shelter for me to live under; God built the shelter for me to live under; God built the shelter for me to live under, he built it on Calvary."

If you ever attended the Flower Hill Baptist Church in Amelia County or the Center Union Baptist Church between the 1950s and the early 1990s, I am sure you remember being blessed by witnessing Rev. Montague singing, shouting and preaching the word of God. Rev. Horace Montague was a tremendous leader in his own right and led countless people to Jesus Christ. From performing baptismal to marriage ceremonies, and then to giving eulogies he was a man of great faith and strong principles.

Rev. Montague was the son of Floyd T. Montague and Nannie Bratcher Montague. This outstanding man was born on the 4th of October in 1921 in the county of Amelia; he was married to Lillian Trent Montague and together they had three children. He decided to join Chester Grove Baptist Church earlier in his life under the leadership of Rev. Seldon Randall. He served in the United States Army during World War II, and after returning home, he surrendered to the call to preach the Gospel. Montague was ordained at Bethlehem Baptist Church in Cumberland County in 1953; he was in ministry there for eleven years. Eventually, he became the pastor of Flower Hill in 1956, which was also one of the churches Rev. Randall had previously pastored. Mrs. Lillian Hicks remembered that Rev. Randall would refer to Montague and his brother Floyd as his sons in the ministry; while at Chester Grove he was the shepherd over Rev. Montague as well as his brother. Horace Montague became the acting pastor over Flower Hill after Rev. Seldon Randall. During Rev. Montague's tenure, he was found faithful by the church members who loved and respected him. He was known for both his preaching and singing; the sermons and songs that God would allow to flow out of him would catch the church on Holy Ghost fire. The song that he would sing most often was "God built the shelter"; this man used to shout down the aisle, telling a story through song, lyric by lyric he would have people of every age on their feet praising the Lord. Center Union Baptist Church and Reed Rock Baptist Church were other places of worship in which Rev. Montague was the pastor over. Keith Evans, a man who was baptized by Rev. Montague, spoke on how he remembers him singing, "I want to go where the thunder don't roll"; others remember him belting out the old-time hymn, "I sure love talking about the Lamb of God." For many, Rev. Montague was more than a great Pastor; he was a great friend and the former moderator of the Amelia-Nottoway-Prince Edward Protective Association. Rev. Montague died on May 28, 1994, but his legacy still lives on.

Rev. Montague and Family

Rev. Floyd Montague

(December 29, 1914 – May 31, 1991)

Rev. Floyd Montague, one of the sons of Floyd T. Montague and Nannie Bratcher Montague was the older brother to Horace Montague. Floyd married a woman by the name of Betty Hobson on April 10, 1937, in Cumberland, Virginia. From their union three children were born: Andrew Floyd Montague, Quentin Leslie Montague, and Deacon Garland Montague; Floyd and his wife were blessed to have grandchildren and great-grandchildren. Much like his brother Horace, Floyd was baptized and joined Chester Grove Baptist church under the leadership of Rev. Seldon Randall. To earn an income he labored as a farmer and also worked as a school bus driver (driving bus #3) for Amelia County Public Schools. For many years Rev. Floyd served as the pastor of Little Bethel Baptist Church, as well as churches located in Nottoway, Buckingham, and Charlotte, Virginia. In his lifetime he led many souls to Christ; needless to say he was a faithful leader not just in his county but throughout Virginia. When Rev. Montague was preaching the gospel, ministers were often underpaid due to the church not being able to afford to pay them. However, this did not deter Rev. Floyd Montague from delivering the true word of God he did what the Lord called him to do; he was well known and appreciated by many. Rev. Montague gave his all to carry the Gospel of Jesus Christ, and he should always be remembered as one of the great leaders of his time.

Little Bethel Baptist Church was founded in the early 1800s by former members of Bethia Baptist Church. For years, services were held in a barn until the first church was built. Mr. Woodrow Pegram, who was an electrician, installed the electrical wiring within the church; however, a second church was built years later. A few of the previous pastors of this incredible church were: Rev. Merritt, Pastor Thomas, Pastor West, Pastor Floyd Montague, Rev. Frank Tyler, and Rev. Hill. In fact, Rev. Hill became the pastor of Little Bethel Baptist Church in 2000 and is still the shepherd over the house

Mary P. Jackson

Mary Patterson Jackson was the daughter of Sarah Watkins Patterson. Mary lived in the Mannboro section of Amelia County and was the wife of the late Edward Jackson. The two of them had a large family, and together they had eleven children. Not only did Mary and her husband raise their children but they also raised their grandchildren as well. Mary was a faithful member of Manassas Hill Baptist Church and her youngest daughter, Shirley Jackson, tells of how her mother was a praying woman; she may not have had a lot of education, but she knew the bible. She was a hard-working, and determined mother who spent her earlier years working in Richmond and also at Fort Pickett in Blackstone, VA. Although Mary did not drive, she refused to allow that to stop her from adding to the household income. With the determination that she possessed she would leave home early, walking to work until someone stopped to give her a ride to Fork Pickett. This woman worked so diligently that she was able to save her money and purchase her own property. Mrs. Jackson taught her

children the importance of saving their money and investing it correctly to take care of themselves. She was faithful to her children and grandchildren; because she was wise with what she had, Mrs. Jackson was able to leave an inheritance to her children upon her passing. Shirley adored the way her mother cooked and expresses how great of a cook she was; she remembers how her mother would prepare homemade biscuits with every meal and each Sunday she would cook a pot of beans along with a homemade cake. Mrs. Jackson also proved herself to be a significant friend; especially, to her neighbor Mrs. Frances A. Thompkins, who is the mother of the outstanding educator, Joyce Medley. Mrs. Thompkins was just as faithful of a friend to Mrs. Jackson as she was to her, so much so that she would take Mrs. Jackson's children to worship at Oak Grove Presbyterian Church and help them out any way that she could. Mary was anchored down in her faith and firmly believed in the power of prayer; her daughter most fondly remembers her walking around the yard praying fervently. She feels that it was those prayers and the grace of God that has kept her family to this day.

Joshua "Josh" Booker

Josh, the son of Fred Booker and Rebecca Hyde Booker, was born in Amelia; and he was raised in the Promise Land area of the county. He had many siblings whose names were: Julia Booker, Robert Booker, Mary Jane Booker Green, William Booker, Rebecca Paige, Amanda Booker Pitchford, Adele Booker Jones, and William Booker. On February 3, 1938, Joshua married a woman named Daisy Daniels; Daisy was a native of Buffalo New York. Records show that Rev. Henderson had the honor of officiating their wedding. In addition to spending much of his time as an active member of Mt. Olive Baptist Church Josh also held several jobs throughout his life. He was employed with the railroad, he worked as truck driver, and he was hired to work at a mill; whatever he had to do to provide for his family. Josh Booker had several children and many descendants; in fact, one of his sons, also named Joshua Booker, has a park in Amelia that is named after him. The Hyde and Booker family is a huge family that extends across the Globe.

Rev. Seldon Peyton Randall

(April 4, 1870 – April 11, 1955)

Rev. Seldon P. Randall, the son of Peyton and Kate Randall, was born and raised in Powhatan, VA; birth records show that he was born on April 4, 1870. He was also married in Powhatan to a Ms. Martha Smith on August 2, 1899. Together the two of them have three children: Peyton, John, and Alfred Randall. Although Rev. Randall only received a fourth-grade education the Lord used him mightily for his Glory. He was the pastor of several churches; however, two of them were Chester Grove Baptist Church and Flower Hill Baptist Church, both located in Amelia, VA. When he was the pastor of Chester Grove Baptist Church, he served there from 1909-1955. He was a dedicated leader with an impactful sermonic delivery; a true shepherd to his flock, he led many to the creeks and ponds to perform their baptismal. As a pastor, he also had the pleasure of marrying many of his members and the responsibility of burying countless others.

Frank Tyler Sr.

(1905 - 1971)

Frank Tyler, Sr. was born in the county of Amelia to Matt Tyler and Annie Johnson. At one point Mr. Tyler was employed by a farm known as the Wood Farm, which was once located on the same land where the Amelia Wildlife is today; in addition to working as a farm hand, he was employed as a funeral director at the Frank B. Tyler Funeral Home.

Having the desire to become an entrepreneur, Frank decided to open his own store in which he called Tyler's Store. Mr. Tyler enjoyed the sport of baseball, and so he started his baseball team within the community where he resided. Needless to say, he was quite active within the county as he also was a committed member of Pleasant Grove Baptist Church where he served as a Trustee for 55 years.

Frank Tyler Sr. with his son Frank Tyler, Jr.

Lucy Harris Tyler

(September 13, 1911 – March 25, 1998)

A teacher and a friend

Lucy Tyler was born in Richmond, VA to John and Estelle Harris and was educated through the Richmond Public Schools. She first graduated from Armstrong Normal School, and then had the opportunity to further her education at Virginia State and Virginia Union University. In the late 1920's she became an educator and began teaching in Amelia County where she eventually met Frank Tyler. Lucy and Frank decided to marry and were wedded in 1932; from this union, two children were born: Irma Henderson and Frank Tyler, Jr.

Mrs. Lucy taught for many years at Brick Church School and Russell Grove School where she taught 7th grade. In 1961 she was honored with being voted the Teacher of the Year. After teaching for a total of 40 years, she eventually retired in 1971; Mrs. Tyler was considered to be one of the best teachers in the county. The Tyler's worked as a team within each other's endeavors, so much so that Mrs. Tyler assisted her husband at his store, funeral home and on the farm. She was also a faithful member of Pleasant Grove Baptist Church where she served as pianist for over 55 years.

Their son Deacon Frank Tyler Jr. is carrying the legacy of both of his parents today—he also currently resides in Amelia. Frank Jr. is the founder of Russell Grove Alumni Association which preserves the history and legacy of Russell Grove School as well as African American history within the county. The Alumni Association also sows into the future of our youth through their scholarship fund. With the help of Ms. Sylvia Hicks and others, the association organizes reunions for the alumni of Russell Grove, schedule meetings and plans specific events. Ms. Hicks is the keeper of the Russell Grove Museum, located in Amelia, and it has artifacts that are well over 80 years old. This would not be if it weren't for Deacon Frank Tyler Jr. and his efforts in making sure African American history is remembered and honored. We support and stand with Mr. Tyler's vision as Russell Grove Alumni move forward to even greater things in the days to come.

Annie Mondrey

A Pillar of the Community

The eldest resident of Amelia County

Mrs. Annie Mondrey was born in 1917 and was reared in the Lodore area of Amelia County; she attended Lodore School and was educated by a teacher named Alice Tyler. The name of Annie's mother was Hallie Gilliam Booker, but she was raised by her grandparents, Rev. Edmund Gilliam (a former slave on the Oaks Plantation) and Hallie Carter Gilliam. At the age of 101, Mrs. Mondrey continues to be a pillar within her family and her community. Even though she was well over 100 years old, her memory seemed to be sharper than ever. I learned so much from speaking with her; she told me of how she remembers her grandfather, Edmund Gilliam, preaching at various churches such as Beulah Baptist, which still stands today on Route 360 in Chesterfield, VA. Mondrey had fond memories of him leaving for church on Sunday mornings in his wagon and returning home late in the evening. At an early age, she remembers being baptized in a water branch near Flower Hill Baptist Church, where she also joined under the leadership of Rev. Seldon P. Randall. Mrs. Annie grew up in a time when racism and prejudice were at its highest. Unfortunately, she also carried the memory of racist incidents that occurred with her family. As a child she overheard her grandparents discussing how her uncle, Jesse Gilliam, was forced to leave his home after clapping his hands at a white woman. As the story goes, evidently this white woman reported him to a few white men in the neighborhood, and they became enraged. The racist men devised a plan to hang him, but thankfully, one of Jesse's white friends informed him of the plot. Jesse Gilliam decided to immediately leave town to make his way to Richmond, VA where he stayed with his aunt. Eventually, Jesse moved from Richmond to Connecticut, where he remained until his death. Mrs. Mondrey had a clear memory of his body being brought back to Amelia in a coffin.

Annie was married to the late William "Stiff" Mondrey Sr., who lived from 1912 to 1993. Together they had fifteen children: Sarah Mondrey (died as an infant); William James Mondrey who is married to Deaconess Lois P. Mondrey; Mary Mondrey Jasper who was married to the late Walter Jasper; Louise Mondrey Harris who was married to the late Charlie Harris; Rev. Nancy Mondrey Clarke who is married to Deacon William Clarke; Martha Mondrey Smith who was married to the late Junius Smith; Estelle Mondrey Banks Tillmon (deceased) who was married to James Banks (deceased)—Estelle Mondrey later married Rev. Tillmon; Audrey Mondrey Caison who married Hollis Caison; Augusta Mondrey Thornton who is married to Deacon David Thornton; Thomas Mondrey (deceased), Paul Mondrey, Victor Mondrey, Andrew Mondrey, Marilyn Mondrey who is married to Deacon Garland Hicks; and finally Maxine Mondrey. With such a large family all hands needed to be on deck when it came to providing for them. So, Mrs. Annie worked several jobs; she was employed with Katherine "Kitty" West, Mrs. Doll, the Leistra family, and lastly she earned an income by cutting corn stacks in Mr. Johnny Lewis's field.

Mary Mondrey Jasper, one of the daughters of Mrs. Mondrey, has many childhood memories of her mom and I was blessed to have her share some of those with me. Mary, reflecting on her childhood told me that her mother was really big on discipline and because of that she was a great disciplinarian. Mrs. Annie made sure she instilled in them the importance of respecting their elders and minding their manners. During the time that she was being raised Mary explains how things were different then— children didn't talk back to their parents and they said, "Yes ma'am and no ma'am. She stated that Mrs. Mondrey did not tolerate a disrespectful child; she kept a dogwood switch in the corner of her house and would use it when they were disobedient. However, Maxine Mondrey, who is the youngest child of William and Annie, said that she never got a spanking. She was a wonderful mother and raised her children to have values and integrity; not only was she a loving mother to her biological children but others as well. Rev. James Taylor, Elder Emanuel Hyde Jr., and countless others consider Annie to be a second mother to them. This woman was well loved and blessed to have lived long enough to know her grandchildren, great-grandchildren, and her great-great-grandchildren.

Down through the years, Mrs. Mondrey established a reputation for her impeccable cooking skills, and she would make the best rolls and preserves in Virginia— her dinners were unmatched. Since the time I was a child until now, I have always looked forward to eating her homemade jelly and pickles. So many families, friends, and ministers have sat and dined at her kitchen table. I will always remember her for being so incredibly welcoming. Over the years, she spent hours sharing with me her history and the history of those who lived long ago. Mrs. Mondrey lived a beautiful life; one that didn't come without its occasional trials and tribulations, but all along the way God was a present help for her. With such a large family and so many who loved her, they always took great care of her. Mrs. Mondrey went on to be with the Lord after 101years of life. I thank God for having known Mrs. Annie Mondrey..

Pictured with Mrs. Annie: Mary Jasper (daughter), great-granddaughter, Aryn Jasper (Victor Mondrey (son), Paul Mondrey (son), Louise Harris (daughter), Annie Mondrey (daughter).

Mondrey Family

First row: Maxine Mondrey, Louise M. Harris, Augusta M. Thornton, Annie Mondrey, William Mondrey, Marilyn Hicks, Audrey Caison, Martha M. Smith. **Second Row:** Andrew Mondrey, Mary M. Jasper, Estelle M. Tillman, Victor Mondrey, Rev. Nancy M. Clarke. **Third Row:** Thomas Mondrey, William Mondrey Jr., and Paul Mondrey.

William "Stiff" Mondrey

Annie Mondrey

Grandparents of Annie Gilliam Mondrey

Rev. Edmund Gilliam

Hallie Carter Gilliam

Rev. Edmund Gilliam was the son of Theolophius and Harriet Gilliam; his parents were slaves of Nathaniel Harrison, and their names are listed in his Will along with the Jeters' and other families. After Nathaniel's death his wife Frankey, who was a mixed freedwoman, became the owner of the Gilliam family. Hallie Carter Gilliam was the wife of Edmund, and the daughter of Moses and Betsy Carter.

Mrs. Anne Mondrey with grandson Rev. Junius Smith Sr.

Lester Randall

A Giant of Civil Rights

Lester Randall, a World War II Veteran and Civil Rights Activist, was born May 26, 1921, in Amelia County. He was one of eleven children born to Lewis and Matilda Wilkinson Randall from the Truxillo community of this county. The first thing that I noticed upon meeting Mr. Randall is that he is a man full of wisdom and strength. Even at the age of 97, his memory is fully intact, and he can recall the days of old as if it were yesterday. He remembers his father working as a farmer and constructing several buildings and homes in Amelia County, including The Hindle Building. His family was quite active in the church; his parents were faithful members of Union Branch Baptist Church and his paternal grandfather, Armistead, served as a trustee. As one can imagine Lester's parents kept him in church, he would attend Union Branch as well, in the old building that was later dismantled; a new one was later built on the same property. Things were different then, Mr. Randall shared with me his memories of the church; the first thing he reflected on is how the church didn't have electricity only lamplights. He remembered that when he was a child, Mr. Kimmiloo Barley was the musician at Union Branch and how that place of worship served as a refuge for many and was one of the meeting places for the Amelia Chapter NAACP. Years later Lester eventually began to serve as the trustee at Union Branch and did so for many years. Growing up in the Truxillo area of Amelia he started his formative education at Truxillo School. The teachers at that time were: Helen Harris, Edith Cooper, and Mozelle Swann. In 1933 he joined the NAACP, and as previously mentioned he became one of the great leaders within this county. Lester reflected on working side by side with his friend Oliver Hill to provide free bus transportation to African American students; he has always fought for the equality of blacks in Amelia. Transportation was not offered to African Americans, in fact, the first time Lester rode a school bus was to a basketball game in Charlotte Courthouse, VA in the 1940's. He served in many organizations working with people like Pat Cousins, Patricia Booker Brown, Andrew B. Wingo (the husband of Mrs. Estella Wingo), Geneva Richardson, and many others to changes the lives of minorities.

In 1947, Mr. Randall married the love of his life a woman from Clarion, PA named Thelma King. From their union, they had four children: Leslie Shelia Harris, Crystal Liggons (deceased), Cameron F. Randall Turner and Waverly Randall. His wife, the late Thelma Randall (September 14, 1929 – June 22, 2018), labored right beside Lester in all of his endeavors; she assisted by fixing meals for civil rights worker, volunteering in the Amelia Chapter NAACP and working actively with the Voters League. She was employed for several years in the Amelia County Public Schools cafeteria. In one of the several interviews that I was honored to have with Mrs. Thelma Randall, she told me that white men would say to her, "We don't like Lester Randall, but we respect him. Lester stands for what is right." As a phenomenal motivator, Lester was also instrumental in the hiring of the first African American employee in the Commissioner of Revenue office. In addition to that, he encouraged the first African American to run for the Clerk office within the Circuit

Court. He worked for many years with C-PAC and received five awards for his accomplishments. Many began to recognize him for what he was doing for the community; so much so that he won an Award of Appreciation from Governor Allen several years ago. This is a man who kept his hand on the plow and never remained stagnant. For a period Mr. Randall found the time to work at the Amelia Sunday School Union. As a provider to his family, Lester worked as a bricklayer with the well-known bricklayer, the late Alexander Wingo; he was also a tobacco farmer for many, many years. During the summer months, he would hire employees; namely Mrs. Rosa Broadnax and her children worked the fields. Mrs. Broadnax's daughters, Lorraine and Rosetta Broadnax, remember their mother going to the fields and tying tobacco for Mr. Randall.

During the creation of this book, I was blessed to have the opportunity to sit with Lester and listen to him reflect over the old days. I can honestly say this book would have been incomplete if it wasn't for the assistance of Lester and Thelma King Randall. Mr. Randall, thank you for being the outspoken and courageous individual that you are. It takes courage to do all the things he has done for Amelia County—Lester Randall is an unsung hero.

Lester and Siblings

Lester receiving an award

Award of Appreciation

Lewis and Matilda Randall

Thelma and Lester

Three years before I met Lester Randall I was told by Rev. Paul Wilson that he would be the one who could assist me with uncovering more about my family history. Throughout the years I was unable to get in contact with him so imagine my surprise when I unexpectedly met him in April 2018. With the assistance of Zavonda Parrish, I had the pleasure of meeting Mr. Randall and speaking with him about my family's history. I'm pleased to say that he was impressed with how much I knew about the history of Amelia County; however, I was even more impressed with him and the wealth of knowledge that he held. A lot was discovered that day; Mr. Randall learned that he and I are related through my grandmother, Alice Granger Hyde. In this photo, I am showing him our family ties through my third book Moseley Echoing Winds Whispers Messages of the Past which he, his parents and other family members are mentioned. Lester confirmed to me that his grandmother is indeed a Granger. Lester Randall was an incredible help, and I am thankful that he was willing to sit down with me to share his wisdom.

Emanuel Hyde III and Mr. Lester Randall

Mrs. Randall with child

Mrs. Thelma Randall

Crystal Randall Liggons

The early days Lester and family

Deacon Henry Foster

The Definition of a Man

A man who has stood the test of time, Henry Anderson Foster has held on to his faith over the years and remains steadfast. At the age of 93, his memory is wonderfully impeccable, and he graciously took his time to speak with me about the past and the people who helped make Amelia what it is today. Without question, he has been a great leader in his own right and has all the makings of being an excellent role model.

Deacon Henry Foster was born on January 8, 1925, to the late Henry and Lillian Smith Foster. His father worked as a farmer and served in World War I. Deacon Foster grew up in a God-fearing household and his father was faithful to his church and community. His grandfather Eli Foster, who worked as a blacksmith, was a slave on the Alfred Anderson Plantation. Deacon Foster has been a long time member of Chester Grove Baptist Church; he considers the day he chose to serve God as a day that he will never forget. It was during a time when pastors would visit the homes of church members to join them for Sunday dinner; on that particular Sunday, Rev. Seldon P. Randall (the former pastor of Chester Grove) came to his parent's home to fellowship and enjoyed a good meal. Deacon Foster says that it was on that day that he decided to accept Christ as his personal Savior. Growing up on the family farm and walking to school are all things that Mr. Fosters has a sharp memory of. It wasn't unusual for people to take shortcuts by maneuvering through the woods to make it to their destinations. Mr. Foster tells of how he and his siblings would always walk through the woods to get to the school; his teacher at that time was Ida Norman. He eventually attended Russell Grove High School and was a part of the 1943 graduating class. After completing high school, Mr. Foster entered the United States Army and served from June 15, 1943, to June 27, 1945; due to health issues, he was medically discharged. As a soldier in World War II, he served as a Private First Class in Company B, the 183rd Engineer Construction Battalion. During his time in the Army, he was stationed in England and says that it was such a beautiful place. After being discharged Mr. Foster vividly recalls, on the trip home, asking God to allow him to be a spokesperson for the people, and God honored his request. Once he returned to Amelia, he started farming, growing tobacco and other crops he would hire school children and their parents to work for him. Three years after being discharged from the Army, Mr. Foster married Ms. Betty Wingo on December 30, 1948; Rev. S. P. Randall performed their wedding ceremony in Amelia, VA. Together the two of them had six children: Henry L., Ralph, Lorraine, Denise, Cindy, and Terri Foster. Deacon Foster was not a man who liked to sit still instead he always kept busy doing what he could for his community. He served two terms as the president of the Russell Grove P.T.A, he was also the president of the Amelia County Branch of the NAACP; and was the president of the Amelia County Sunday School Union. His list of accomplishments doesn't stop there; the list is quite long.

He served as Treasurer on the Amelia County P.T.A.; was a board member of the A.M.P.C (Area Manpower Planning Council), the Virginia Balance of State Planning Council, St. Mary's Health Care Center Advisory Committee, and The Amelia Telephone Corporation Board of Directors. Foster was elected to the Amelia County Board of Supervisors in 1971 and served as Chairman of the board in 1981. When he was needed he helped as the vice chairman, chairman, and co-treasurer of the Amelia County Democratic Committee. He also served on many other boards in Amelia County. He is currently a member of the Obadiah Bethany Lodge No. 170, the Amelia County Branch of the N.A.A.C.P, The Amelia Democratic Committee, and is still an active member of the Chester Grove Baptist Church. At Chester Grove he serves as a deacon as well as a trustee; he has been a Chairman of the Deacon board for over 45 years. He is also active in Sunday school at Chester Grove where he once served as a teacher, co-superintendent, and treasurer. For a period Foster ran his dry cleaning business which was called Foster's Dry Cleaners in Crewe, VA; he closed it down in December 2005. In 2007 he was the Amelia County Christmas Father and was awarded the Citizen of the Year Award by the American Legion Post 87 in 2014. Deacon Foster was inducted into the Amelia County Hall of Fame in 1977 and was the first African American elected to the Amelia County Board of Supervisors.

 At 93 years young, Deacon Foster says that he still has more to accomplish; jokingly he stated that he has another twenty more years of work to do. My response to him was, "Sir, you have done it all." In an impromptu interview, I asked him, "What would you say to the young people today?" He quickly answered, "I would tell them you can be anything you want to be." I salute Deacon Foster for the incredible life he has lived and for all that God has allowed him to do.

Deacon Foster

Deacon Henry & Betty W. Foster

Foster Family

Deacon Henry Foster and his siblings

Raymond Wilson

(February 14, 1900 –June 22, 1976)

Raymond Wilson was born the son of Rev. Jeff and Margaret Langhorne Wilson in the Mattoax area of Amelia County. He attended what was known as the Community School of Brick Church which was situated behind the old Liberty Baptist Church. At the early age of nine, after completing the second grade, Raymond quit school and began working to add to the family's income. According to his son Edwin, Mr. Wilson worked for several employers in the county. Those employers were Dr. Rucker's Farm, Mr. and Mrs. Mason (in their tobacco field), and lastly, he was employed as well as taught the skill of carpentry by Royal Hyde and became a talented carpenter.

Raymond was the husband of Louise Johnson who was the daughter of Harrison Hyde and Josephine Johnson Brown. The couple had seven children: Ethel Wilson Johnson (deceased), James "Tee" Wilson (deceased), Estelle Wilson Green, Eliza Wilson Jones, Clarence Lee Wilson, and Edwin Wilson. Raymond was considered to be a firm father, a hardworking man and very intelligent, especially for an individual who only received a second grade education. Wilson and his wife were quite devoted to their family; so much so that they raised their grandson James "Junnie' Wilson Jr. and had a helping hand in raising their grandson, Arnold Wilson. Unexpectedly, he became the community barber and ultimately started his own makeshift business. He started cutting hair with hand clippers and perfected his technique so wonderfully that people in the neighborhood would travel by any means necessary to have their hair cut. When he first became a barber, he would charge each customer 35 cents per cut and extra for a razor shave. As time went on Wilson purchased a pair of electric clippers, and his prices gradually went up to $1.00 per cut. This man was quite skillful in everything that he did teaching himself a lot as he went along. I learned that he even taught himself how to work on guns and how to make his own gun stock. Still, he continued with his barber profession until his passing in June 1976. He was very well known and respected in the county.

Kimmiloo Barley

(1902 – 1987)

Kimmiloo Barley was the son of the late John Henry and Frances Johnson Barley; he was an educated man who graduated from the Virginia Seminary School out of Lynchburg, VA. When he finished his schooling, he taught at Morven School and substituted at Brick Church School located in Amelia County. In his lifetime he served as a farmer, teacher, and a musician; he was indeed a man of many gifts and talents. Mr. Barley could build an instrument out of anything, including a handsaw. He volunteered his time as the pianist/organist at many of the churches in Amelia, including Flower Hill and Chester Grove Baptist Church, where he served for 50 years. He was the husband of the late Pearl Goodman and together they adopted several children.

James Archer

(July 2, 1926 – March 21, 1997)

James Archer was born on July 2, 1926, and was the son of William and Sallie Baker Archer. Victoria Robinson, the daughter of Leon Robinson and Lucy A. Robinson, was his wife; and from their union, three children were born: James Archer Jr., who married Nancy Epps; Sylvia Archer (deceased); and Joan Archer Owens, who married Deacon Eyser "Ike" Owens. James Archer was a determined, business-minded individual who was the proprietor of James Archer and Son Landscaping, established in Amelia County. For a period he also owned a store and added to his income by hauling pulpwood. James was a hard working man who was not only committed to his family but was also dedicated to serving this country as he fought in the Korean War and was a proud Army Veteran. As his health began to fail towards the later part of his life, he continued to work as much as he could. The children and grandchildren of this man both loved and respected him to the fullest. James was a member of Mt. Olive Baptist Church where he served as a trustee. He was a great man and will never be forgotten

Pictured upper left: James and Victoria Archer

Roger Hicks

(October 30, 1919 -1988)

The son of Elijah and Perline Lacy Hicks, Roger Hicks, was born in 1919. He was inducted into the United States Army, on August 28, 1942, when he was just 22-years-old; he served this country faithfully until April 2, 1945. Several years later, when he was 30-years-old, he married his wife, Lillian Elizabeth Harris on March 7, 1949, in the county of Amelia. From this union, five children were born: Roger Hicks Jr., Garland Hicks, Ernestine Hicks Scott, Brenda Hicks Johnson and Sylvia Hicks. To earn an income Mr. Hicks worked at a sawmill owned by Martin Heath, and for many years as a bus driver for Amelia County Public Schools. He was a faithful member of Liberty Baptist Church where he was a deacon for many years.

Dr. Henry Featherston

(1940 – 2018)

A Champion for all people

Dr. Henry Joseph Featherston was born on December 21, 1940, to Henry Featherston Sr. and Mary Mays. He was a 1958 graduate of Booker T. Washington High School and later earned a Bachelor of Science degree in 1963 from Norfolk State College. Dr. Featherston furthered his education even more by obtaining a Master's Degree from American University and Longwood College, in 1971; lastly, he studied at International University where he received his Ph.D. On August 35, 1961, he married the late Rosa Benton and together they raised three children: Adrienne Redd (who is married to Carlton Redd); Dana Brown, and Anne Weaver (who is married to Glen Weaver).

Dr. Featherston came to Amelia to teach at Russell Grove High School; while there he taught Math, Business, Drivers Education, and Science classes (he also served as Science department chair). For a period Dr. Featherston was both the football and basketball coach, but his interest was not only in sports; he was also fond of music and was responsible for establishing the first black band in Amelia and served as band director. Over the years Dr. Featherston experienced promotion and became the Administrator Assistant to the Superintendent; next, he was elevated to an Advisory Specialist and director of the Title 4 program. As time went on Featherston moved up the ladder, proving to be a great asset to the field of education; it wasn't long before he was given the position of Associate Principal, then Assistant Principal, and finally the role of Principal of Amelia County High School. In the late 1990s, he also served as the principal of Amelia County Elementary school. After some years had passed, Dr. Featherston decided to return to the school board office to serve as an Assistant to the Superintendent. The one thing that can be said about this great man is that he genuinely had a heart to help where ever he could make a difference. His labor included working as the Director of Educational Service, the Director of Secondary Education, and as the Director of Transportation. He was appointed to the school board in 2006 and served as chairman in (in or until??)2008. Due to his passion, he aided on many other boards including the Amelia County Industrial Development Authority and the Russell Grove Alumni Association.

Along with his other achievements he was also a published author. In his early years, when he came to Amelia Dr. Featherston joined the Zion Hill Presbyterian Church where he remained faithful until his passing. I can certainly say that this man has been highly regarded and honored throughout the years of his life. In February in 2018, Dr. Featherston was honored by several churches during their black history month programs. One of his last awards, the DWC Leadership Award, was presented to him by Pastor Tara Owens and the Destiny Worship Center Youth Leaders on

February 27, 2018. On that day Featherston spoke on the days of segregation and how when he would order food from a restaurant he'd have to go to the back door to be served. He informed the congregation of the racism he experienced up close and while in his travels; he was one of the great individuals who paved the way for everyone who has come after him. Personally, he encouraged me to continue to move forward with researching and writing; he also permitted me to use his books as references for my work, and I am eternally grateful. Featherston paved the way for me as an African American author in the county; because of him, the foundation has been laid in Amelia for African Americans to walk on the road to success. On May 8, 2018, Dr. Featherston went on to be with the Lord, his homegoing service was held at Hope Chapel in Amelia. Many came from far and near to pay homage to the man who has done so much for so many; without question, his work and legacy will be remembered.

Dr. Featherston upper right with Russell Grove High School band 1967

Dr. Featherston at Russell Grove School in 1968

Pastor Tara Owens presenting Dr. Henry Featherston, with the *DWC Leadership Award* (2018) at Destiny Worship Center's Annual Black History Month Program.

Alice Rosebud Tyler Mabry

"A Life Well Lived"

(May 30, 1927 – October 20, 2017)

Alice Tyler Mabry, affectionately known as Sis, by her family and friends was born on May 30, 1927, in Amelia County. She was one of two children; her father was Edward Tyler, and her mother was Alice Pitchford Tyler. Her brother, William Tyler, served in the U.S. Military for several years and was married to Mary Robinson, who was the daughter of Leon and Lucy Archer Robinson. From the union of William and his wife Mary, Mrs. Mabry became the aunt of their daughter, Chermine T. Booker. Chermine is the mother to two children and the grandmother to several grandchildren and great-grandchildren. Her children's names are Jerry Mondrey (deceased) and Iollette Mondrey. Alice Mabry's father who was nicknamed, "Bubba" worked as a farmer while her mother was employed as a teacher at Lodore School, Morven School, and Promise Land School. Her mother even had the opportunity to work closely with the influential Maggie Walker in the St. Luke Insurance.

Mrs. Mabry was an educated woman as well; in fact, after graduating from Russell Grove High School in 1944, she later attended Virginia State University where she received both her Bachelors and Master's Degree in Education. Once she received her degree, Mabry began her career as an educator at Russell Grove, where she taught until 1958. However, she didn't leave Russell Grove for too long; she returned in 1960 to continue teaching for an additional year. On June 9, 1951, Alice married a man by the name of Theodore W. Mabry Jr., and together they raised two children: Theodore Mabry Jr. and Quentin O. Mabry. At one point in her life, she moved to Lynchburg, VA where she devoted 21 years to educating the students within the Lynchburg Public School system. She later became a Volunteer Director of Continuing Education and an instructor at Virginia University in Lynchburg. Participating in many organizations including the NAACP Mrs. Mabry received many accolades for her hard work and dedication in education. Indeed, she will be remembered for years to come for her incredible achievements; and her legacy has been well preserved by her sons, her granddaughter (Alyson), and her niece, Chermine Tyler Booker.

Wishing *Alice T. Mabry*, a Zeta, much success with the 2013 Virginia State Leadership Conference

The Mabry's, Theodore Sr., Theodore Jr, Quentin, Katrina and Alyson
Lynchburg, Virginia 24502

Courtesy of Mabry Family from Zeta Conference

110

Sister-in-laws: Mary Robinson Tyler and Alice Tyler Mabry

Niece: Chermine Booker

Photos courtesy of Chermine Booker and from the late Alice Mabry (Facebook page).

Father & Mother of Alice Tyler Mabry: Edward and Alice Pitchford Tyler

Alice Mabry brother and family:

William Tyler, Mary R. Tyler and Chermine T. Booker (child)

Chermine Booker

Chermine & family

Chermine Booker

Jerry Mondrey

DeCara Mondrey

IyLahna & mother Iollette

Jerry Mondrey

Macon Booker

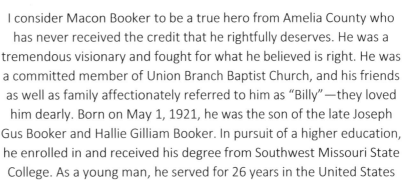

(May 1, 1921 – January 16, 2008)

A Champion

I consider Macon Booker to be a true hero from Amelia County who has never received the credit that he rightfully deserves. He was a tremendous visionary and fought for what he believed is right. He was a committed member of Union Branch Baptist Church, and his friends as well as family affectionately referred to him as "Billy"—they loved him dearly. Born on May 1, 1921, he was the son of the late Joseph Gus Booker and Hallie Gilliam Booker. In pursuit of a higher education, he enrolled in and received his degree from Southwest Missouri State College. As a young man, he served for 26 years in the United States Air Force. After Macon retired from the military, he returned to his hometown in Amelia County. Upon his return, he began serving on different boards and committees in the county, including Amelia Parks and Recreation; the CPAC; the NAACP Democratic Party; the Amelia-Nottoway Department of Social Services; and on the Board of Supervisors for District 1 for several years. Macon, as well as others, were instrumental in making changes within this county. Receiving the approval to have the Virginia Veteran's Cemetery in Amelia County was one of his primary goals. He made many trips to Washington, D.C and attended multiple board meetings to ensure that the dream of having a veteran's cemetery within the county would become a reality. I can remember having several conversations with Mr. Booker while at his sister, Annie Mondrey's, home. He always showed an interest in current events and often discussed with me the importance of obtaining an education. Many of his accomplishments today are unspoken in Amelia, but it shouldn't be that way because of the efforts that he made to improve the lives of people who reside in this county. Mr. Booker was married a total of three times; his second wife, Mrs. Olivia Harris Perkins Booker, was born in 1930 and died in 1995. After the passing of Olivia, he married a woman by the name of Dr. Beatrice Booker, who was a long time educator and school board official.

Olivia Harris Perkins Booker was the daughter of Joseph and Vera Harris out of Amelia, VA. She was a faithful member of Flower Hill Baptist Church and is the mother of Debra Wilkerson (who is the wife of Glen Wilkerson). Mrs. Booker was employed with the Amelia County Public Schools system where she worked as a school nurse for 14 years, retiring in 1993. Everyone knew her to be a loving person who honestly had a heart for children. During her career as the school nurse, she treated a variety of conditions and minor injuries with the help of assistants such as Mrs. Lola Anderson. She wasn't only the school nurse, but she also acted as a surrogate mother to dozens of children. Students would go to her seeking advice, and she was always willing to lend a helping hand or merely serve as someone to talk to. Before retiring she was entered into the Amelia County High School Hall of Fame for her service to students in the school system

Leon Robinson

(April 5, 1907 - March 5, 1976)

Leon "cheese" Robinson Sr. was born on April 5, 1907. His father was Deacon Amos Robinson, and his mother was known as Gary "Gay" Robinson of Amelia County. Chermine Booker, the great-granddaughter of Amos and Gay, remembers her great-grandparents and the big house they lived in. She tells the story of how her grandma Gay kept a basin in the kitchen— referring to a time when they didn't have running water or electricity. The basins would be filled with water and used as a sink.

Leon joined Mt. Olive Baptist Church at an early age; his father, Amos was a deacon there. Like most African Americans who grew up in the early 1900s, he didn't have the opportunity to receive a quality education. Although Mr. Robinson only received up to a fifth-grade education, he was a very wise man. Leon was the husband to Lucy Helen Archer Robinson, and together they had nine children. For many years Leon worked at the sawmill in the Mannsboro area of Amelia to support his large family. His daughter, Shirley R. White, remembered her dad would ride to work with his brother Herman "Mike" Robinson. She states that several workers, from the Royal family, would catch a ride with Mike, taking a seat in the bed of his truck. People were all about helping each other out, especially during those times. Much of Leon's time was also spent working his farm at his home where he not only raised chicken, pigs, and cows but also tended to his vegetable garden. Many who knew him said that Leon was a man of very few words who would say what he meant and always meant what he said.

Lucy Helen Archer Robinson

(November 12, 1912 – February 12, 1980)

Lucy was the only daughter of Tom and Elizabeth "Eliza" Bland Archer. She was reared in the Promise Land community of Amelia; at an early age she was baptized and joined Promise Land Baptist Church. Her husband's name was Leon Robinson and once married to him she became a housewife. Lucy was known for her excellent cooking and specialized in preparing homemade rolls. It is said that Lucy would rise early in the morning to prepare meals for Leon to take to work. Although she had to manage a large family she always kept her home clean and intact; Lucy didn't take any mess from her children and also raised her nephew, Henry Archer, as one of her own. Mrs. Shirley Robinson White, the daughter of Lucy, remembers how her mom would keep a long green switch that she had no problems using when they were disobedient. Mrs. Robinson was a mother who demanded respect, and that is what she was given. Shirley also remembers her parents did not regularly attend church, but they would often send the children. Although Lucy wasn't a regular church attendee, her daughter states that she still believed in paying tithes to her home church, Promise Land Baptist. When Shirley's parents would send her to church, she recalls that she and her siblings mostly attended Mt. Olive Baptist. The fond memories that Mrs. Robinson's daughter has from attending Mt. Olive is how she would see so many coming to church in cars, or by horse and wagon. She also remembers her aunt, Annie Belle Robinson would sing in church from the depths of her soul. Baptism for the Robinson children wasn't held indoors like it is today; Shirley remembers walking through the woods to a creek and receiving her baptismal there. After it was over,

they had to walk back to Mt Olive Baptist, and the journey was not a short one. All of the children of Leon and Lucy attended Chula School, and many attended Russell Grove High school. Leon and Lucy enjoyed life and had a special love for their children and their grandchildren. Reminiscing on her childhood, Remy, the granddaughter of Mr. And Mrs. Robinson, can vividly recall her grandmother singing in the kitchen while she prepared meals for the family; in fact, Remy also remembers how her grandmother would always cook a hearty breakfast that included fried pork, molasses, and eggs. During the week the favorite dish that she would prepare was beans and homemade biscuits. Sunday dinners were always special as she would often fry chicken, make potato salad, greens, homemade cakes, and pies. As a housewife, she developed a weekly routine while on the weekends the family would come together to hang out. On Mondays Lucy would wash clothes and hang them on the line; between

Tuesday and Wednesday she would take those freshly washed clothes and iron them. Chermine Booker, another grandchild of the Robinsons, tells of how Lucy would iron clothes for a white family in the Chula community her technique was to use starch and a cast iron that had to be heated on the stove. Lucy's Thursdays would consist of performing a complete house cleaning; as a housewife her days were busy. Remy states that Saturdays were her grandmother's days to get dressed up and venture to the Louise Archer store where she would relax and enjoy the company of others. However, there were other Saturdays when the Robinson's would take a ride to Broad Street in Richmond to handle certain errands and with them would be Chermine and her parents William and Mary Tyler. Chermine says they would usually stop by Standard Drug Store, Troy's Store, and then Murphy's Store where they would purchase bologna, bread, and coca cola.

Children and grandchildren of Leon and Lucy Robinson:

1) Mary Elizabeth Robinson Tyler (May 1927 – 2012) who was married to William Tyler—they had one daughter, Chermine T. Booker.

2) Victoria Robinson Archer married James Warren Archer on April 26, 1947—they had three children: James Archer Jr., Sylvia Archer (1950-2018) and Joan Archer Owens.

3) Dorothy Robinson was married to the late Roosevelt Robinson—they have seven children: Dorothy Estelle Robinson Corum (Deceased), Remy Robinson Corbett, Connie Robinson (deceased), Roosevelt Robinson, Richard Robinson, Cinderella Robinson, and Walter Robinson (deceased).

4) Rachel Helen Robinson Hyde (December 13, 1932 - January 12, 1998) who was married to Howard B. Hyde Sr.—their children are: Carolyn L. Hyde Carroll, Lucy Hyde Ross, Howard Hyde Jr., Mary Hyde Harris, Clinton Hyde and Clyde Hyde. Rachel also raised the children of her brother-in-law Emanuel Hyde Sr.,

5) Richard Robinson Sr. (January 23, 1935 - August 28, 2012) married Marian Mason on July 16, 1955. *For a list of the children of Richard and Marian Robinson Sr. please reference the Richard Robinson section of this book on page 133.*

6) Beatrice Robinson Alston has two sons Russell and Thomas.

7) Shirley Robinson White who married Raymond White Sr. on September 17, 1954. Raymond served in the US army and was a Trustee and Usher at Promise Land Baptist Church. The two of them had eight children: Mildred White Royal, Ronald White (deceased), Raymond White, Sharone White, Jefferson White, Michael White (deceased), Maurice White and Deleah White.

8) Deaconess Vernell Robinson Royal who is married to Elwood Royal Sr. — they have two children: Rev. Cynthia Royal Simms and Elwood Royal, Jr.

9) Leon Robinson who was married to Rosa Pitchford Robinson— their children are: Sharon, Angie, Elsie, Leon Robinson III, Jordan, and Jennifer.

Several generations of descendants from Leon and Lucy extend across the globe. I thank Shirley and Deleah White for all their help and sharing their memories of Leon and Lucy Robinson. I also say thank you to Chermine Booker and Remy Corbett for blessing me and sharing with me the story of your grandparents. The memory of Leon and Lucy Robinson is held in the hearts of all that knew them.

Son-in-law Raymond White and Lucy Robinson

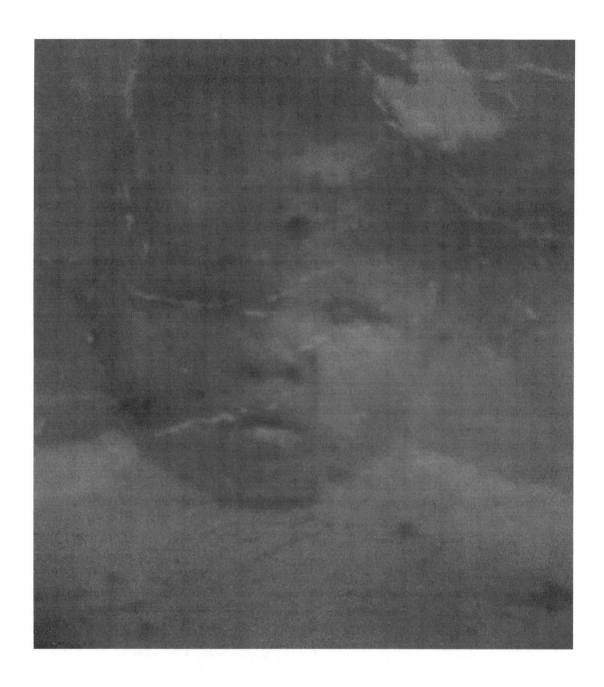

Lucy Archer Robinson baby picture in 1912

Mary Tyler, Lucy A. Robinson, Leon Robinson Sr., Richard Robinson, Victoria Archer, Dorothy Robinson, Rachel Robinson Hyde, Vernell Royal, Leon Robinson Jr., and Beatrice Alston.

Daughters of Leon and Lucy Robinson:

Victoria Archer, Mary Tyler, Dorothy Robinson, Marian Robinson (wife of Richard Robinson), Shirley White, and Rachel Hyde.

Siblings of Leon Robinson

Herman "Mike" Robinson and wife Annie Belle Robinson

Isaac Robinson

Descendants of Leon and Lucy Robinson...

These two have many descendants and it would be close to impossible to obtain pictures of everyone from this extensive family; however, thanks to Mrs. Shirley White, Chermine Booker and others I was able to include the following photos.

Deacon Elwood and Vernell Royal

Rachel Hyde and others

Anthony Robinson

Elwood Royal Jr.

Rachel R. Hyde

Shirley R. White holding grandchild

Leon "Buddie" Robinson

Victoria and Lucy Robinson

Vernell R. Royal

Remy Corbett

Richard Robinson

Joan Archer Owens

Pam Robinson

Vernell and Deacon Elwood Royal Sr.

Deacon Elwood and Vernell Royal

Rev. Cynthia Royal Sims, Vernell Royal and Paris Allen

Shardae, Elwood Jr., Shirley, Deacon Elwood Sr., Vernell, Rev. Cynthia and Paris

Richard Robinson Jr   Chermine Booker   Mary and Lonnie Harris   Sylvia Archer

Cynthia and Paris   Clyde Hyde   Lucy Hyde Ross

Carolyn Hyde Carroll   Michael White   Shirley & Elwood Royal Jr,   Raymond White Jr.

And Leon Jr.

Walter Robinson   Howard Hyde Jr.   Pastor Tara Archer Owens

Pam, Rashid, Ramond, and Shiccarra   Michael White   Pam, Rashid, Ramond, &Shiccarra

Garland Sr.Deleah, LaTeshia,   Joan Archer Owens   Clyde, Clinton and Howard

Mike and Garland Bannister Jr.

Sylvia Archer   Shirleeta Turpin   Clyde Hyde   Ronnie and Remy

Mildred W. Royal and Deleah   Dorothy and Roosevelt   **Deacon James Archer Jr.**

Rodney, Eyser Jr. and Eric   Barry Archer and Tertia Archer

Shirley Robinson White

Mrs. White has been a great asset to this project, sharing her knowledge of the past and her memorabilia. I thank God for her and all she has done to contribute to this body of work. At 80 years young she is still one of the pillars of her family; they loved her well, and I am grateful to have even known her. Shirley was the wife of the late Raymond "Teddy" White.

Shirley at Mt. Olive (sisters)

Deleah White

Shirley & Victoria

Raymond "teddy" White

Min. Emanuel Hyde III and Mrs. Shirley White

Richard Leon Robinson Sr.

(January 23, 1935 - August 28, 2012)

Richard Robinson was the son of Leon and Lucy Archer Robinson. In his youth, he was a student at both Chula and Russell Grove High School. Although he did not complete high school, this man was quite intelligent. Mr. Robinson was a man of many talents; he found work as a mechanic and was employed at several shops in his lifetime. Ironically, although he did not graduate from high school he was given the opportunity to teach, and did so at Russell Grove High School; he was even offered a job at the Amelia-Nottoway Vocational Center in which he had to decline. There was nothing that he could not do, even without a complete education, he succeeded in many tasks and duties in this life. The gifts that he was born with indeed made room for him as he was offered jobs and positions that he didn't necessarily have the proper education for or certifications needed.

One of his greatest talents seemed to be wrapped in mechanics; for a period of time he was co-owner to and worked at Booker's Garage in Richmond, VA. He worked on vehicles for years and earned a reputation for being one of the best. Even after his health began to fail, that didn't slow him down, Mr. Robinson could tell you anything about fixing cars or trucks. He was so good that he didn't have to move, he was able to simply direct someone on what to do. Remy Corbett, the niece of Mr. Robinson, tells the story of how on one particular occasion her mother was having issues with her car and Mr. Robinson came to the rescue. Mr. Robinson along with his son Richard Jr. stopped by, and from a chair, his father directed him to everything to do to fix that car. They made it look too easy. Richard Robinson also worked for Smith Logging; while he was employed there, he was featured in the Richmond Times-Dispatch for cutting down a tree that many feared, because of its split, was too dangerous to remove. He fearlessly cut the tree without a problem. Regardless of the health challenges that Robinson faced, he never allowed them to defeat him—he was a fighter until the end. He was a great family man and was loved dearly by his wife Marian, their children, grandchildren, and great-grandchildren. "Poppa" is what he was affectionately known as by his family; and many say that the apple didn't fall far from the tree, because much like his father Leon, Mr. Robinson said what he meant and meant what he said. His wife, Marian, was a faithful helpmate to Richard until the end of his life. She was and is the rock of their family and thankfully is still alive and well today. Although Richard passed away in 2012, his memory will never be forgotten

Children of Richard and Marian Robinson: Shirleeta Garnett, Richard Robinson Jr., Darlene (died as a baby), Michael Robinson Sr., Tony (died as a baby), Pamela R. Jefferson, Anthony Robinson, Gloria Robinson and Taylora Robinson.

Richard and Marian

Mrs. Marian Robinson

Children of Ricard Robinson Sr.

Taylora, Gloria, Pam, Marian, and Shirleeta

Shirleeta Robinson Turpin

Strong and Selfless

Although born in New York, Shirleeta was raised in Amelia County by her maternal grandparents, Carl and Elizabeth Mason. She graduated from Amelia County High School in 1974 and went on to receive a higher education with a focus in Nursing. Once Shirleeta completed her education she began working as a private duty nurse for over 30 years. Within her family Ms. Turpin started a family tradition in which she gave her children names that began with 'Shir,' and she gave her nieces and nephews names that started with 'Sha.' In every way, Shirleeta adored her family and was considered the rock of the family supporting each of them and keeping everyone united the best way she could.

Unfortunately, Turpin was diagnosed with bladder cancer but survived it for 15 years. She endured her sickness like the true soldier that she was and truthfully was always more concerned about other people rather than her own medical issues. Regardless of what she faced she never complained; she raised and cared for her two daughters, who suffered from sickle cell anemia; and another daughter who battled her share of illnesses and the loss of her precious baby boy, Phillip. Without question, Mrs. Turpin was the perfect example of what a great mother is. Sadly, she passed away on January 3, 2016, leaving behind her husband Steven Turpin and their four children: Shiromecco Garrett, Shirmanda Turpin, Shirnae Turpin and Corey Young.

Racell Broadnax

A True Survivor

Racell Broadnax is a woman of strength, who despite facing many obstacles has stood firm through it all. She acknowledges the power of God, his strength, grace, and mercy that has kept her throughout the years. Racell was born to the late Virginia Ann Broadnax and was reared in Richmond, VA. She was raised by her mother, and grandmother, the late Rosa Margaret Broadnax, along with the help of her aunts Elsie, Lorraine, and Rosetta. Early on she was taught the importance of taking care of herself and was raised to have strong morals and self-respect. On July 25, 1992, life as she knew it changed when a drunk driver hit her family in a head on collision while driving in Amelia. Virginia, her mother; Elsie Broadnax, her aunt; Rosa Margaret Broadnax, her grandmother; and Amzi Broadnax, her cousin were all killed in this horrific accident. It was Racell and her cousins Ameisha and Ricky Lamont Broadnax who survived the accident. At the time of the incident, Racell was sixteen and Ameisha was only three-years-old, and both were in critical condition.

For two days, Racell was in a critical state with life-threatening injuries; she suffered from a broken leg, a broken femur bone, a broken arm, facial injuries and internal bleeding. Once she woke up from the comatose state, it was immediately explained to her the death of her loved ones. Again, Racell was only sixteen years-old when all of this occurred, and as she got older, she had to rely on God to see her through it all. The prayers of her loving aunts, uncles and other family members helped her to persevere. Within herself, Racell knew that she had to fight and not give up; she understood that her cousin Ricky was depending on her to keep her head up and as hard as it was, that's what she did.

Due to the facial injuries acquired from the accident, her doctors explained that she'd have to receive plastic surgery to correct it; in addition to that, she was told that she would never be able to have children. However, God had another plan He healed the wounds that were on her face and she never once had to have plastic surgery. The blessings didn't stop there when doctors said it would never happen, God said it

would, he healed her body and today she is the mother of four blessed children; two daughters, who are business owners and two sons. This young woman is an overcomer, when speaking with her she said something so simple but profound, Racell noted, "Even through grief you have to move on." She has learned that having faith in God can see her through any challenge. Racell and her cousin Ameisha were unable to attend the funeral of their loved ones; however, the service was recorded, and she was able to watch it later on. She vividly remembers Rev. Ryland Robinson saying, as he was finishing his sermon, "Our loss is Heaven's gain, this is to be continued." Certainly, it takes courage to experience what Racell has gone through, and I know that it has been by God's grace that she has made it this far.

The vehicular accident that occurred on June 25, 1992, in the county of Amelia took the lives of four members of the Broadnax family. So many residents of Amelia who knew this family were devastated over the death of these four individuals. Rosetta Broadnax, a daughter, sister, and aunt of the deceased remembers that day well. As she reflected during my interview with her, she spoke about how she remembers it being extremely hot, yet she and her family planned to attend a horseshoe tournament in the Red Lodge Community within Amelia. Rosetta decided to ride with her friend Sandra Massenburg, Bubbie, and her sister Lorraine "Stella" Broadnax to the event; meanwhile, her sisters Elsie "Minnie" and Virginia "Jenny", her mother Rosa "Tuda", her niece Racell, her nephew Amzi, and her son Ricky piled into a separate car together with the intention of also attending the tournament. Sadly, just a few miles away from the event, their vehicle was hit head on by a drunk driver, and four of them lost their lives. Days later, after their passing, thousands of people gathered together on the grounds of Amelia County High School to say goodbye to Tuda, Minnie, Jennie, and Amzi. The funeral was held in the high school gymnasium; I was eleven-years-old at the time, and I remember attending the service with my mom. I will never forget sitting in the bleachers of the school gymnasium during the service and seeing the preachers and leaders who came to support the Broadnax family. The gymnasium was filled, and due to limited seating, many were unable to make it inside; however, they showed their support and condolences by standing outside, sitting in the field or waiting around the school in hopes of saying goodbye to the ones whom they loved so much.

Racell pictured at the MADD victim board in honor of her deceased family members.

136

Rosa Margaret Butler Broadnax

(June 19, 1931 – July 25, 1992)

Rosa was affectionately known as "Tuda," she is the daughter of Sam Butler and Ida Anderson. On November 4, 1950, Rosa married Mr. Henry Thomas Broadnax. The couple had seven children: Eddie "Mike" Thomas Broadnax (deceased), Elsie "Minnie" Mae Broadnax (deceased), Sam "Rocky" Henry Broadnax (deceased), Virginia "Jenny" Ann Broadnax (deceased), Lorraine Broadnax, Rosetta Broadnax and Robert Lee Broadnax. Rosa and her husband also helped raise his brother, Marvin "Luke" Broadnax, and a nephew, Paul Monroe. Rosa's husband, Henry Thomas Broadnax, was a hard-working man who drove an 18 wheeler log truck for Mr. E.F Chimney. While Henry worked outside the home, Rosa worked has hard within the home as a homemaker handling the day to day activities with their seven children. Henry played baseball on Frank Tyler's team and would often walk from his home, near Kitty West Store to Frank Tyler's; and later he would send for someone to pick up his entire family to watch their games. After Henry's untimely death, in 1966, Tuda who was no stranger to hard work took care of her family to the best of her ability. She was able to find work with several white families and also in tobacco fields. After the passing of Rosa's husband her daughter, Lorraine, says that she specifically remembers family friends Deloris Banks, Mrs. Eloise Banks (mother of Deloris), Leslie Banks (brother of Deloris), Mike Banks Jr., and Mary Jane Banks (Sam's Godmother) visiting her mom to make sure she was doing well. Rosa "Tuda" also experienced an untimely death as she passed in an automobile accident in 1992. Tuda's presence has been greatly missed by everyone who knew her; Evelyn Harris was the closest friend to her (Rosa was the Godmother of Evelyn's daughter Donna Lee Harris) and remembers well how Tuda would walk to her home every morning to visit. Mrs. Evelyn says that before she'd leave to go back home, she would often say, "I gotta go home to put a pot on the stove" she was a wonderful cook, often preparing meals for not only her family but occasionally their friends as well. When times were tough, as it was for others during that period, she would make a meal out of almost anything, including pork and beans. According to Lorraine and Rosetta, their mother was sweet and loving, but she didn't take mess from anyone. In an interview with Racell, she stated that her grandmother whom she affectionately called, "Momma" was her everything. Racell also agreed that her grandmother was a loving and God fearing woman who would give the shirt off of her back for anyone. For Ricky Broadnax, he describes his grandmother as honest, sweet, caring and a woman who did whatever she could for her grandchildren. Rosa Margaret Butler Broadnax left a huge impact on her family and had a love for them that was unconditional. I honor the life of this woman; continue to rest in peace Tuda

Rosa Broadnax holding her daughter, Rosetta

Elsie Mae Broadnax (April 9, 1952 – July 25, 1992) was affectionately known as Minnie. As a youth, she attended Amelia County Public Schools. Her sister Rosetta Broadnax remembers Elsie as being a very personal person and a real sweetheart. She was very close friends with Mary Ann Person and Janet Jackson Cousins. Elsie took great care of her children and loved her family immensely. The Broadnax family holds fond memories of Minnie. Racell, a niece of Elsie, says that although she was her aunt, she thought of her as another mom. Ricky Lamont Broadnax remembers his aunt Minnie used to pick with on him about having big knees. The overall census is that she was a jokester and a lover of life. Her family considered Elsie to be very wise and knowledgeable about a variety of things and she is missed even to this day..

Amzi Broadnax (July 24, 1978 – July 25, 1992) the son of Elsie "Minnie" Broadnax was named by his Aunt Stella, after an older cousin. Stella and Rosetta Broadnax both remember Amzi as being a sweetheart with his unique personality. As a student at Elkhart Middle School, he was a big brother who loved his little sister Amiesha. Racell says that he was more of a brother to her than a cousin; and although it was tragic losing so much of her family on the same day, it was especially difficult losing Amzi. He died just one day after his 14th birthday; Racell often wonders what his life would have been like if he was here. Ricky, a cousin of Amzi, also says that he was more like a brother to him as well. He tells of how the two of them were together just about every day. Although he could be a bit slick, Amzi didn't play with his mom Minnie. Whenever he misbehaved, he would get the kind of spanking that some kids need today. Ricky attended Elkhart Middle School as well, and he remembers returning to school, after the accident, and being shown so much love and support; many mourned the death of this young man.

Virginia Ann Broadnax (April 13, 1955 – July 25, 1992) was affectionately known as "Billy" by her friends and family. However, Rosetta and those who best knew her simply called her "Jenny." Her sister Rosetta remembers Jenny well and would usually see her with a cigarette hanging from her mouth. Virginia was a good person and was loved by many. Racell Broadnax was the daughter of Virginia, and she remembers her mom as being a beautiful, quiet and laid back individual.

The Broadnax Family

We Remember Them

Rosa "Tuda"

Elsie "Minnie"

Virginia "Jenny"

Amzi

Ricky Lamont Broadnax

A True Survivor

Ricky is one of the survivors of a 1992 vehicular accident that took the lives of four of his family members and is the son of Rosetta Broadnax. In an interview with Ricky, he shared with me many memories that he has of his family. He has a vivid memory of the day in which the accident occurred; they were on their way to a horse show when his Aunt Minnie, who was driving stopped by her best friend Mary Person's house first. As they began to make their way up the road to the show, Ricky says that he remembers the song "End of the Road" by Boyz II Men playing in the car. The last thing that Ricky has a memory of is his Aunt Minnie saying, "What is that fool doing?" referring to the car that was heading towards them. The next memory that he had was waking up in Johnston Willis Hospital. This survivor was knocked unconscious by the impact of the collision, after only receiving a concussion and a few minor injuries Ricky was discharged from the hospital the next morning. He explained that the next memory he had, was of him waking up at home in his bedroom and hearing a lot of people talking in the other room. After waking up, he went into the bathroom, saw his swollen face in the mirror and immediately began hollering for his mom. It wasn't long after that moment that he started to ask for his grandmother, whom he lovingly called momma. Rosetta broke the news to him that his grandmother died in the accident, this devastated him. A few days later, he attended his family's funeral; for many years the accident affected him in various ways, but like Racell he could not give up. Ricky relocated to Amelia (began attending Amelia County High School) and stayed with his Godmother, Anita Jasper; for a period he also lived with Mrs. Delia, James, Sam, Davin and Tasha Patrick. In the past years, Ricky has proven himself to be a fantastic father to two children and a hardworking man. Although he has suffered much loss, he understands that God spared his life because he has a plan for his life. For over two decades I have known this man, and I consider him a great friend and brother to me; I know that his story is far from being fully told. I am excited to witness all of what the Lord will do in and through Ricky Lamont Broadnax.

Rosetta & Ricky Broadnax

Antoine & Ricky

Rosetta and Lorraine

Sam, Loretta, Rosetta & Robert Lee Broadnax

Rosetta & Lorraine

Lorraine, Sam & Rosetta

Betty Ann Banks Person

(July 16, 1950 – June 5, 2014)

A Virtuous Woman

Betty was born and raised in Amelia County to the parents of Ernest Banks and Sarah Evans; however, she was reared by her adopted mother, Annie Banks Jackson. Betty attended Brick Church School and Russell Grove High School where she graduated from in 1969. At an early age, she accepted Christ and became a devoted member of Liberty Baptist Church. Later she relocated from Amelia to Richmond, VA, and although her church membership changed, she never forgot Liberty Baptist. On December 19, 1979, Betty married a man named Richard Person; she was a loyal wife and a devoted mother to their children: Reytina Banks, Dana Banks, and Latoya Person. She also treasured her grandchildren: Phillip Irvin, Diamond Banks, and Dana Banks. Betty was one of the most anointed singers of her time. She had a pure and robust contralto voice that could soar high, very similar to the famous Mahalia Jackson. Where ever she would sing whether at church or just at home the room would be filled with the Glory of God. I remember when I would see her name on church programs on the days when I was required to sing I would feel some kind of way because she was so incredible I never wanted to sing after her; she would usher in the Holy Spirit with her God-given voice. The church would be on fire in such a way that the only thing that would be needed after her song was the benediction. Indeed the most requested song for her to sing was "Jesus how I love to Call Your Name" some people in the congregation would fall out, others would cry, and a number of them would shout, including me. Other songs that she would often sing were, "Walk with me" and "May the work I've done speak for me." On one occasion, many years ago, I asked her what her secret was to singing the way she did. She smiled and said, "It's the anointing that makes the difference." Over the years she has sung in many churches both within a group and as a soloist; without question, she was a fantastic Minister of Music. Mrs. Betty even appeared in plays but only went where she was spirit led. Betty had many offers to be a recording artist, but she turned down every offer that she was presented with. Her desire wasn't to sing for money her only desire was to sing for the Lord. This woman didn't merely sing the gospel, but she lived it. Betty had a way of finding the good in everyone; she never had a bad word to say about anyone regardless of what they said or did. As she honored the Lord with her life, she also served as an intercessory prayer warrior. She loved her family especially her siblings, nieces, and nephews. Mrs. Betty was a special angel to everyone who knew her or had the great opportunity to hear her sing unto the Lord. On a more personal note, although she is no longer here, Betty will always be a great inspiration of mine; she is a role model who had patience like Job. Truly the work that she has done speaks for itself.

Proverbs 31:10-22, 25-30 reads like this: "Who can find a virtuous woman? For her price is far above rubies. The heart of her husband doth safely trust in her, so that he shall have no need of spoil. She will do him good and not evil all the days of her life. She seeketh wool, and flax, and worketh willingly with her hands. She is like the merchants' ships; she bringeth her food from afar. She riseth also while it is yet night, and giveth meat to her household and a portion to her maidens. She considereth a field, and buyeth it: with the fruit of her hands she planteth a vineyard. She girdeth her loins with strength, and strengtheneth her arms. She perceiveth that her merchandise is good: her candle goeth not out by night. She layeth her hands to the spindle, and her hands hold the distaff. She stretcheth out her hand to the poor; yea, she reacheth forth her hands to the needy. She is not afraid of the snow for her household: for all her household are clothed with scarlet. She maketh herself coverings of tapestry; her clothing is silk and purple. Strength and honour are her clothing; and she shall rejoice in time to come. She openeth her mouth with wisdom; and in her tongue is the law of kindness. She looketh well to the ways of her household, and eateth not the bread of idleness. Her children arise up, and call her blessed; her husband also, and he praiseth her. Many daughters have done virtuously, but thou excellest them all. Favour is deceitful, and beauty is vain: but a woman that feareth the LORD, she shall be praised. Give her of the fruit of her hands; and let her own works praise her in the gates."

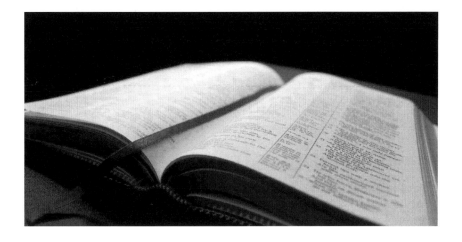

Betty and her grandchildren

Pastor Tara Owens.

A Leader after God's Heart

How can we hear without a preacher and how can they preach unless they have been sent?

Pastor Tara Owens is the daughter of the late Sylvia Archer and the granddaughter of Victoria Robinson Archer and the late Mr. James Archer. She was raised in Amelia, VA and attended Mt. Olive Baptist Church; she received her education from the Amelia County Public Schools and was a graduate of Amelia County High School. On May 27, 1989, Pastor Tara Owens married the love of her life, Deacon David "Tony" Owens, Sr.; they were blessed with three children whose names are: David Owens, Jr., Shamika Owens, and Dustin Owens. In addition to that blessing, God has also made them the grandparents to four girls. Pastor Tara, lovingly known as "Pastor T" by her congregation, answered the call that God has over her life back in 1998 and has been living for God ever since.

At a time when there were few women ministers in Amelia, she still pressed on to do God's will; in fact, she was mentored by one of the greatest female evangelist to come out of this county, the late Evangelist Odell V. Monroe Johnson. After many years of teaching and preaching, in 2014 God gave Pastor and Deacon Tony a vision of a new ministry that He desired to be in Amelia County— and Destiny Worship Center was birthed. Pastor T was called to be a Pastor and became the founder of Destiny Worship Center, also known as DWC. Services were first held at the Obadiah Lodge within the county, and it was there that she and Deacon Owens remained faithful, preaching the word of God and ministering to the needs of God's people. In 2015, Pastor T had the honor of baptizing 14 individuals on the same day; it was no doubt that God was moving through that ministry and touching the hearts of those who entered into the church. Presently, she has been blessed to baptize over approximately 50 people and has led many to Christ. Due to the steady growth of the congregation worship services were eventually moved to the Veteran's Center, also in Amelia County. A little while later DWC moved again, to its present building, formerly known as Epps Assembly Hall, on Winterham Road in Amelia, VA. Through the grace of God, I have witnessed many being saved, delivered and set free under this ministry.

Pastor T is a Godly leader, and an exceptional mentor who doesn't compromise the word of God—she speaks it the way that God tells her to, nothing more and nothing less. This is a woman that truly has a heart for the people of God, and she is always willing to help wherever she can; she has even had the opportunity to officiate several wedding ceremonies while in ministry, including the wedding of her eldest son David Jr. and his wife, Amber Booker Owens. Destiny Worship Center is a progressive church that follows the move of God and has been blessed to have many members; in fact, I am grateful to say that I am

147

one of them and I serve as a Minister under the shepherd of the house. I can testify that my spiritual parents, Deacon Tony and Pastor Tara Owens, only seek to do the will of the Father; these are people who pray for us, sacrifice for us, and war for us in the spirit. We at DWC proclaim that we are imperfect people serving a perfect God and we press toward the mark for the prize of the high calling in Christ Jesus. We can see that God is doing a great work through this ministry and we believe that He will continue to do so as we follow His lead. To God Be the Glory for all the things He has done and all that He has in store for Destiny Worship Center.

Owens Family

Deacon Tony and Pastor Tara   Deacon Tony, Pastor Tara, Dustin, Shamika, and David Owens Jr.

David Jr. and Dustin   Deacon Tony and David Jr.   Deacon Tony, Pastor Tara, Dustin,Shamika and
David Owens Jr

Take me to the water...take me to the water...take me to the water to be baptized

Kneeling: Pam Robinson, Christian Robinson, Latasha Owens, Aleasia Watson, Alisha Nicole Nash, Darlene Robinson, Charlene, Rasheeda Thomas Standing: Yvette Weathers, Joyce Owens, Jessica, Shamika Owens, ZaVonda Parrish, Diane Dickerson, Rosetta Broadnax, Allison Owens, Delice Wingo, Andrea Banks

Pastor Tara and Mother Gladys Broadnax

DWC

New Testament Gospel Singers

The Spirit of Worshippers

Font row: Deacon Sean Archer and Harry Brown Jr.
Second Row: Martin Owens, Rev. Lawrence Owens, Deacon Tony Owens, Deacon Wayne Johnson, Terrance Mosby, and Pastor Christopher Owens

New Testament is one of the many gospel groups out of Amelia County that has been carrying the message of Jesus in song for several years. God uses New Testament for His glory and through their music he touches the hearts of his people. They are true worshippers who believe in ushering in the presence of the Lord through praise and worship. The current members in this anointed group are Minister Lawrence Owens, Pastor Chris Owens, Deacon Tony Owens, Martin Owens, Shauntrice Owens who is the daughter of Mr. and Mrs. Chris Owens; Harry Brown, Deacon Wayne Johnson, Deacon Sean Archer, Terrance Mosby and Vincent Mondrey. Each group member is a leader in his or her own right and is faithful in their churches and communities. Throughout the years they have been a blessing to many by using their gifts and talents to the Glory of God.

The Owens men who are in the New Testament are all brothers who started out singing in Promise Land Baptist Church; they are the sons of Mr. Lawrence and Correntha Epps Owens, the Epps families primarily worshipped at Promise Land Baptist. Their mother was very influential in inspiring them to use their God-given voices. Mrs. Correntha was the daughter of Sidney Epps and Correntha Pleasants; she hailed from the Epps family in Amelia which was and still is known for their excellent singing ability. Years before the New Testament Gospel Singers group was formed, Mrs. Correntha had her own group called, the Inspirational Gospel Singers. The Owens brothers and their sisters Rev. Pinkie Royal, and Rev. Josephine Jackson were all a part of that group; other members were Nancy Epps Archer, Virginia Scott, Marjorie Owens, Herbert Butler, and Mary Ann Epps Hansboro.

New Testament was birthed out a men's group that came together for a Men's Day program at Promise Land Baptist Church. The group met at Deacon Eyser "Ike' Owens house, and it was there that Deacon Central Jefferson named them New Testament. The founding members of the group that were assembled for the Men's day program were Pastor Chris Owens, Deacon Eyser "Ike' Owens, Clifford Wilkinson, and Herbert Butler. After the program, New Testament became an official group sharing the gospel through song, the members of the official group were: Pastor Chris Owens, Deacon Eyser "Ike' Owens, Herbert Butler, Deacon Central Jefferson, and Deacon Tony Owens; Pastor Lawrence Owens and Martin Owens joined the group a later. Throughout the years the Lord has blessed the group tremendously; they have ministered throughout Virginia and traveled out of state on various occasions.

In an interview with some of the members of New Testament, I asked them what the key to their group's longevity was. The answer, given by Pastor Chris Owens, was prayer, he states that not only do they worship together, but they also pray together before every rehearsal. The group is dedicated to the great commission, the call of God. Each of them agreed that within New Testament there are no big I's or little U's, they each have a sincere respect for one another and cover each other in prayer.

When I asked the group what would they say to younger people who are pursuing the gospel music ministry they replied, "Ministering in song has to be what God has placed in your heart to do." Pastor Chris Owens said, "There will be great challenges but know that God has called you to do it. You should always minister with the anointing, allowing God to order your footsteps." He also said, "Allow God to use you in every situation, go out with intensity whether you have drums, a pianist or just yourself. If you perfect the instruments of your voice you will have instruments to glorify God; sing to win souls for Christ." They referenced the scripture that reads, "Seek ye first the kingdom and His righteousness and all of these other things shall be added unto you." It is evident that this is a scripture, that as a group and as a family they have lived and continue to follow to this day. I thank God for the New Testament Gospel Singers

New Testament at their 20th anniversary celebration (taken over 10 years ago).

Antoine "Saratoga" Jackson

The Man, the Music, & the Legacy

As a child, Antoine was surrounded by music. His earliest memories are the sounds of music being played from his grandmother's eight track by legendary artists such as James Brown, Roy C, and other southern soul singers. He vividly recalls, his grandmother, Mary Ann Jackson, playing music while she was preparing Sunday dinner. Little did Antoine know, that year's later people would be playing and enjoying music that he produced. The musical seeds that were planted in him early began to take root and produce fruit. When reflecting on moments from his childhood, Antoine remembers Sam and his friend Terrance "Tee" El would sit around and rap. Sometime later Sam began to perfect his rapping gift; at one point Antoine's older cousin, Mark Crowder, came down from New York to visit and he and Sam would sit on the picnic table in front of Sam's mother's home writing and playing music. Inspired by his cousin, Antoine would go home and write as well, around that time he says that his cousins did not know how influential they were to him. While in middle school, Antoine tells of how he linked up with Sean Archer and a few others to do a science fair presentation, and for that presentation, they performed a song by Black Sheep, a rap group from the 1980s and 90s. Although he was quite nervous, he remembers they received a positive response from their peers; in fact, even at lunch his peers were congratulating him for a job well done.

That day was a clue to the uncovered talent that was within him. In 1993, during his eighth grade homecoming dance, he recalled standing by the DJ all night while Sam and his group, Show and Tell performed. On that same night, the DJ passed Antoine the microphone, and he gave it his all; as soon as his performance was over James "Jamie" Patrick (Sam's brother) lifted him in the air and the crowd went wild. Many were amazed by his talent, including Sam who did not know he could rap; from that moment on Sam began to mentor Antoine, teaching him everything that he knew. Often Antoine, Tee, and Sam would come together and write music; during a time when most local rappers were recording on karaoke machines, Antoine says that Sam took his money and invested in his own recording sessions. One of the first recordings that Antoine recalls hearing of his mentor was a song was entitled, "Budda's Coming Up" featuring Yolanda Westinghouse. The song was sampled from the hit record, "I'm Coming Out" by the legendary Diana Ross. When he was fifteen-years-old, Antoine's mom, Ella Jackson, gave him some money for him to have his own recording session as well. The first song Antoine recorded with Sam was, "Believe It" which they received positive feedback on. About two years later, Antoine began to collaborate with Victor (VJ) Howell, who was also an aspiring artist, and together the duo formed The Unknown Disciplez. Eventually, he and VJ bridged with Sam, Tee EL, and a young guy named Rashid

Robinson these men called themselves LOTUS, which meant Lyricist of the Unknown Sector. Most often LOTUS recorded at a studio owned by a man known as Scottie boy. In the 90s people were searching for hope, and many were able to find a glimpse of that through Hip Hop. They told stories of their struggles, hopes, aspirations and the day to day realities of what was going on in society. In 1998, when Antoine graduated from Amelia County High School, his mom told him that he had two options, to go to college or join the service. After weighing those options, Antoine decided to join the army with a plan to pay for his education and obtain money to buy his own recording equipment; by 1999 he purchased the recording equipment that he desired. While in the Army, he would visit home as much as he could; during one of those visits he ran into his friend and former classmate, Aubrey "AJ" Mallory (aka Focus) who is a skillful lyricist. The two men conversed about music and Antoine gave AJ one of his tapes. Once AJ played the tape, he thought he was so good that he felt inspired to record with him. Soon after Focus and Antoine began to make music together, Lemark "Markie" Butler (aka Chosen), and Jumar Brown (aka JBrown) decided to come on board with the two of them. Usually, they would come together to record for fun, until one day, a man named Lamar Craft (a cousin of Antoine and Sam) played a few of their songs to his college football teammate, Pless Jones from Emporia, VA. Pless began to ask who these guys were and once he was informed, he made the statement of wanting to manage the group; however, the group still needed a name. It was Antoine that came up with the name Virginia's Frontline, a name that originated from a comment made by one of his Army buddies, Marques Jones, who mentioned that a frontline group should be in each state. So, in 2003 Virginia's Frontline became the official name of this talented group of guys. With Pless Jones as their manager, they signed deals to perform and have performed at many events rocking the show everywhere they went. Under CNI Entertainment Virginia's Frontline recorded the album, In the Line of Fire; a few of the tracks were: Gangsta Mobile, In the Line of Fire, Dem Boyz Out, and Born Soldier. Virginia's Frontline never forgot home and became true trendsetters of Hip Hop in Amelia. They represented Amelia in a way that was never done before and grabbed the attention of a young generation, some who had never heard of the county. Antoine's stage name became Saratoga "Toga," and his stage presence was electric. In a 2009 interview, Antoine said that he refused to be in a box, his music, his life, and style could never be characterized. Since the beginning, Toga has always had the full support of his family. Quite honestly his family (the Dickersons' & Patricks') have always had an unbreakable bond; regardless of where Toga has been in his life, he could always rely on the bond of his family. His mother Ella "Lou" Jackson, Calizza Jackson (sister), his grandmother, and all of his aunts have been great supporters of him, Sam, and the group as a whole. So much was achieved with Sam and the rest of Virginia's Frontline; for example, they have had the opportunity to perform at numerous events and have been interviewed on several radio stations, including WVST 91.3. In addition to that Virginia's Frontline was featured in a documentary about the Rappers of Virginia. On Sunday, August 10, 2008, Sam Patrick and his brother Davin Patrick died in a tragic car accident. It was a day most Amelia residents would never forget and to honor their memory Toga released a mixed tape called, Blood of my Brother, a masterpiece that acknowledged Sam as being the foundation on which he stands on today. In 2009 Toga produced the theme song for the HBO Showtime Comedy, White Boyz in the Hood. It has been years later, and Antoine "Toga' Jackson continues to create the music that he so passionately loves. He is happily married to the love of his life, Nicole Miles Jackson, and together they have six children whom he adores. One of his latest recordings was done in honor of his baby girl, and it is entitled, "Beautiful Fear." While looking ahead into the future, Antoine vows to keep going he says, "Hip hop is a culture, and I love the culture; Hip Hop was first built to stray youth away from the NYC streets that were flooded with gangs." Today, Hip Hop is a worldwide genre and Toga continues to produce, write, style and do what is in his heart to do. If you ever listen to his music, then you will understand his journey. Just as Toga and Virginia's Frontline stands on the shoulders of Sam "Booda" Patrick many other aspiring artists who will come from Amelia will stand on his shoulders as well. So I salute Antoine "Saratoga" Jackson for his perseverance, and I know that one day soon he will be internationally known.

"It's about trying to present something unfamiliar in a familiar way. Relating to people who never met you by being human. All of my emotions and thoughts being on display plus me having fun is key, that's how I approach my music." —Antoine "Saratoga" Jackson

LOTUS: Antoine "Toga" Jackson, Rashid "Godzilla" Robinson, Victor "Genghis" Howell, Sam "Booda" Patrick, and Terrance "Tell" El.

Tribute mix tape to Sam Entitled: blood of my brother

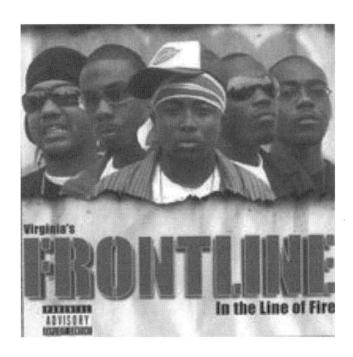

Focus, Chosen, Toga, Booda, and JBrown

Antoine and his wife, Nicole M. Jackson

Toga with the cast of White Boyz in the Hood

I AM...TOGA

Antoine "Toga" Jackson

Dedicated to the memory of Sam "Booda" Patrick & Davin Patrick

Sam Patrick (1974 – 2008) was a father, son, brother and friend. As mentioned earlier he is credited for being the first rap artist from Amelia to record music in a recording session. Sam was a lyrical genius, and he will always be remembered by those who knew him and the music he created. He had such a love for music that he was nicknamed "Wait" because he was usually always listening to music he would make you wait until that song was over before one could talk to him. Ricky Broadnax shared with me many memories of Sam, who was like a big brother to him. Ricky says that Sam was a great person who loved playing jokes on people. ZaVonda Vinson Parrish also holds fond memories of Sam; he had so much talent, that she says he was famous in her eyes and a good friend. Sam broke the mold for many talented rappers from Amelia.

Davin Patrick (December 30, 1980 – August 10, 2008) was a devoted father, son, brother, uncle and cousin. He attended Amelia County Public Schools and graduated from the high school in 1999; while in school he used his talents and was a great basketball player. Davin loved his friends and was a massive supporter of Antoine and his musical endeavors. Ricky Broadnax also thought of Davin as a brother and says, "He will always be my dawg." Mrs. Delia, Davin's mother, was adamant about teaching her children how to cook and take care of themselves. So, it was no surprise that Davin became an outstanding cook reflecting the lessons that his mother taught him. Ricky remembers the day when he and Davin, who were both in 11th grade at the time, came home after school and his mother surprised him with a brand new car. It was a Jetta, and it wasn't long after the initial surprise that Davin installed a deck and put an amp in the back; he loved working on his vehicles. There weren't many who didn't love this young man ZaVonda Parrish says that she looked at him like a little brother. I've personally known him since 1988 when we first met in second grade we remained friends until his passing. May he continue to rest in peace.

Davin and Sam

Pictures courtesy of Antoine Jackson and Latasha Patrick Moon

Frances Dickerson

(July 16, 1961 – August 13, 2016)

A Loving Diva

Frances was full of life and had a big personality— she wasn't afraid to be herself. In her youth she attended Amelia County Public Schools; she was a member of Union Branch Baptist Church. One of her favorite things to do was to dance; at family gatherings, she always had a good time and was loved by her entire family. Frances was as real as they come and she didn't mind speaking her mind whenever she needed to.

God blessed Frances with two sons, Aaron and Quantia Dickerson, who sadly preceded her in death; she loved her children with all of her heart. Frances had a big heart and dearly loved her mom, sisters, nieces, nephews and her entire family. She was another individual who supported Antoine in his musical aspirations; he says that she was like a second mother to him. One of her closest friends, Rosetta Broadnax says that she and Frances were more like sisters than friends and remembered that their friendship began when they first met in kindergarten. Employed as a private duty nurse, Frances was terrific at her job and acted as a fantastic caretaker to her patients. While reflecting on the life of Frances, ZaVonda Parrish summed it all up and said these words, "Frances was a go-getter, a hustler, beautiful, outspoken and was not afraid to be herself." Somehow she could put a smile on the faces of whomever she was around, always letting her light shine. The absence of her presence is felt in the lives of her friends and family, but her memory lives on.

Jeannette Giles Crenshaw

(November 20, 1946 – January 19, 2017)

A Gift of Love

Jeannette Crenshaw was born on November 20, 1946, to the late Arthur and Rosa Giles in the Ammon area of Amelia. Jeannette attended Ammon School and was valedictorian of her graduating class. She also attended Russell Grove High School where she graduated in 1964. Mrs. Crenshaw was a devoted longtime member of Mount Level Baptist Church where, for over 60 years, she served in various organizations including the missionary ministry. The heart that she had towards people was genuine; Mrs. Crenshaw cared so much that she established her own at home ministry in which she would mail cards and poems to the sick within her community and beyond. Altogether she and her husband have three children; many of their children's friends thought of her as a second mother and most of them affectionately called her Mom's C. I had the pleasure of growing up with her youngest daughter Candis, and I distinctly remember Jeannette, her husband Jerry and her mother Rosa being present at just about every school activity that Candis was a part of. For over 20 years she remained a significant influence in my life and until her health failed we remained in close contact, praying for each other often. Every time I asked her how she was doing she would usually respond with a, "I'm making it." She was a very private and quiet woman, but in 2010, after a cancer diagnosis, she began to allow her voice to be heard; she started telling stories of her life while becoming active with the American Cancer Society Relay for Life in Amelia. In 2012, she was nominated to serve as the Life Honorary Chairwoman of 2012. She was featured in the June 7, 2012 issue of the Amelia Bulletin Monitor. Within that same year, I organized my first gospel program entitled, "Bridging the Gap" in which all proceeds earned were donated to the American Cancer Society in honor of Mrs. Jeannette Crenshaw. Jeanette has also had great success with raising money and receiving donations to present to the Amelia Relay for Life organization; she took her task of seeking donations very seriously because she understood how important this cause was. On January 19, 2017, Jeannette peacefully concluded her life's journey; however, the way that she loved her family, her community, the church, and the youth will forever remain in the hearts of those she mattered to the most

Jerry and Jeannette Crenshaw

Delois Henderson Obi

(August 25, 1951 – June 11, 2018)

A Woman of Praise

Delois was truly one of the boldest women of God I had ever seen; she had a passion and zeal for God that was refreshing to see. Mrs. Obi was born the daughter of Deacon Fred and Jennie Mable Mitchell Henderson in Amelia County; she received her education from Russell Grove High School. The FBI employed Delois for four years, and Verizon (formerly Bell Atlantic) for twenty years as an Administrative Assistant. Her relationship with God was genuine, and she didn't mind praising God; amazingly she had a soul winning anointing that was radical. The boldness that she held was incredible, and she had no problem walking up to a stranger and asking them if they knew Jesus. This anointed woman was willing to spread the good news of the Lord anywhere and at any time.

Often visiting different churches Delois, at a moment's notice, would rise from her seat and say "Praise the Lord Saints!" she would then proceed with a sermon, song, scripture or a testimony— whatever was on her heart. She certainly knew how to give God praise; whether it was by running, shouting, or lifting her hands, she consistently glorified the Lord. I can remember being at various gospel concerts in Richmond and seeing her in the front of the church shouting or running up and down the aisles. There was no shame in her; she lived her life to please God and not man. Those who knew her well will never forget the passion that she had for the Lord and his people. Quite regularly Mrs. Obi would visit the sick and the elderly, as God's hands on the earth, she believed in fellowshipping and praying for everyone she visited. Delois was a devoted mother of three and a wonderful grandmother; her children are Denita Horton, Monique Perkins, and Clarence Henderson. In her later years, she met and married the love of her life, Mr. Chinazo Ikenna Obi. On June 11, 2018, Delois was called home to be with the Lord, and I do not doubt that she has surely received her crown. At her homegoing celebration, there were song selections such as, "Going up Yonder" and many others that sent the church into praise. While sitting in the service witnessing the praise of God and the celebration of her life I thought to myself, "What a great service for a great lady." Several family members and friends paid tribute to her life, and so many beautiful things were said about her. I'm sure the angels heard her say, "Praise the Lord Saints" as she reached Heaven's doors. Delois Henderson Obi, I thank you for showing us how to be radical, bold, and resilient when it comes to serving the Lord. Thank you for demonstrating to so many how to praise God in season and out of season.

Minister Marquis Carlisle

A Distinguished Gentleman

Marquis Carlisle was born in New Jersey but was raised in Conway, South Carolina. He graduated from Conway High School and furthered his education at Charleston South University (CSU) in Charleston, South Carolina. During his time at CSU, he pledged for the Phi Beta Sigma Fraternity; around the same time, Minister Marquis lost his best friend in an unfortunate accident. It was the loss of his dear friend that inspired him to enter into a new career as a funeral director. Prior to transitioning into his new career, he worked at a hotel; however, he stepped out on faith and relocated to Virginia to pursue his dream of becoming a mortician. Once he arrived in Virginia he began attending John Tyler Funeral Directory and Embalming School; in 2011, while he was still a student, he started working for the Michael W. Hawkes Funeral Home in Amelia, VA. Since working as a mortician Minister Marquis Carlisle has proven himself to be phenomenal at his craft. He has earned respect and great appreciation from the families that he has assisted during their time of bereavement. Carlisle states that it has been a blessing to work alongside Mr. Hawkes and that he has learned a lot from him. On August 2, 2013, he married the love of his life, Shanice Oliver Carlisle; he is an incredible father of two sons, Keshawn and Josiah Carlisle.

Marquis is a member of Destiny Worship Center (DWC) where Pastor Tara Owens is the shepherd over the house. He serves as one of the Youth Ministers at DWC and preaches with conviction and with a passion for God's unfailing word; there is no doubt that this man is a great asset to the body of Christ at DWC. In looking ahead, Minister Marquis expresses his desire to one day own his own funeral home and continue to work on being the best Godly leader that he can be. When asked what he would say to young readers who will pick up this book he stated, "If you have a dream or goal people might say that you can't push past the odds to achieve them, but you can do all things through Christ that strengthens you." Pastor Tara Owens has dubbed him "The Distinguished Gentlemen" and each time DWC assembles he proves to be just that. I can say that this man is indeed a lover of God, a spectacular brother in Christ, and a wonderful friend. I believe that there will be many things God will give him to meet the needs of Amelia and the world. His natural family and his spiritual family both wait in great expectation to see the continued move of God in his life.

Joey Edmond Vinson Jr.

(July 5, 1954 – May 23, 2000)

Joseph Edmond Vinson Jr. was also known as "Joey" was born on June 5, 1954; he was the son of the late Joseph and Florence Booker Vinson. He was raised in Truxillo, VA where he attended Amelia County Public Schools and was a member of Union Branch Baptist Church.

At an early age, he learned the values of homeownership and entrepreneurship. While growing up on the family farm, he was no stranger to hard work. His father, Joseph Vinson Sr., passed away one month before Joey's ninth birthday. After the death of his father, his mother Florence Booker Vinson, continued to raise him; she was the daughter of a well-known teacher by the name of Annie Johnson Booker. Florence was described as a sweet lady who loved to cook and who had a special love for her only child, Joey, as well as her family. For a period, Florence worked as a maid for Mrs. Chore, but she was primarily a homemaker. Joey's mother was a phenomenal baker and constructed a building on her property where she planned to open a bakery. However, when she recognized Joey's strong desire to become a homeowner, she decided to give the building over to him so that he could fulfill his dream.

Vinson was an incredibly talented individual who used his gifts and talents to advance in life; this man was always self-employed, he never worked for anyone. Like his grandfather Anderson Booker and other men within his family, Joey was a farmer who raised cows, bulls, chickens, pigs, goats, and even grew his garden. As the proprietor of Vinson Construction Company, he was blessed to have several employees while in business. It has been said that Vinson was an excellent employer and treated everyone who worked for his with respect. Most of the men who worked for Joey were longtime friends, some of those men were: Herbert "Big Bird" Trueheart, Maurice Delaney, Derwin Eggleston, and Roy Booker; these men built several homes in Amelia and surrounding counties. Rosetta Broadnax remembers Joey well and told me how he loved a song called, "Follow me" and whenever he heard that song he would immediately start dancing, and everyone would follow along. He had several hobbies that he enjoyed doing, he was an avid hunter, and joined the St. James Hunting Club; he also had a love for fishing. Vinson was an active individual who loved sports and even played for many years on a baseball team in Amelia known as the Paineville Sluggers. Although Joey Vinson passed away on May 23, 2000, his memory still lives on. He had a laugh that was contagious and will always be remembered by those who were closest to him. Joey Vinson has one daughter, ZaVonda Vinson Parrish, who along with her children continues to keep his memory alive.

Annie Parrish and Joey Vinson

Zavonda Vinson Parrish with her father, Joseph "Joey" Vinson

ZaVonda Vinson Parrish

The Eagle Story

ZaVonda is a woman of purpose who has always carried a vision inside of her and is now turning those visions into reality. She has been a friend and a sister to me for over 25 years; I've had the pleasure of witnessing her overcome some of her most significant challenges. She is an eagle, that in this season will soar to new heights. ZaVonda is the daughter of Annie Parrish and the late Joey Vinson. She grew up in a close family; she was surrounded by love from her parents, her grandmother Florence Booker Vinson and her great aunt, Patricia Booker. As a child, she attended Union Branch Baptist Church. When ZaVonda speaks of her father her face lights up, it's clear to see that her love for him runs deep even to this day. As a self-proclaimed daddy's girl ZaVonda admits that she always tried to do whatever she could to impress him. Growing up in the country, she loved the outdoors and could do anything that a boy could, everything from climbing trees to planting gardens. Her mother Annie has been there for her during every season of her life and is her number one supporter. While speaking with ZaVonda, she thought back to her childhood and stated that she never got a spanking as a kid. Another big supporter of hers was her grandmother Florence Vinson who was a truly an added blessing to her life there wasn't anything that Ms. Florence would not do for her granddaughter. Leading into her teenage hers she began styling her hair and by the time she reached the age of fourteen ZaVonda started seeing herself as a business owner.

She moved to Richmond in 1999; however, due to the passing of her grandmother as well as her father within three months of each other, she returned to Amelia. Losing both relatives three months apart hurt her tremendously—unable to cope she began to suppress her grief with alcohol and drugs. Even through these experiences, her purpose began to take form. Following the death of her father she opened a salon called, *ZaVonda's Hair and More*; ironically, she hated styling hair and says that she opened a salon because she knew that it's what her dad wanted for her. Today, ZaVonda admittedly says that "She was living someone else's dream." Even after his death she still had a desire to want to impress him and honor the life that he lived. Still, once the salon was up and running things seemed to be getting better for her, she owned cars, furs, and everything that she needed to have a comfortable life; however, all of that changed in January 2012. It was the month of January when she learned that her stepson, Brandon Baker, was killed in an automobile accident. The pain from that loss was instantaneous and unbearable to her at that time, but ZaVonda explains how God gave her an epiphany and began to work on her from the inside out. Following the death of her stepson, God delivered her from alcohol, and she allowed him to transform her life; still, she had to go through the process of being refined for her God-given destiny. At one point ZaVonda had lost hope and contemplated death, but once again the Lord rescued her and showed her who she was in Him through the word of God. During that time she created the Brandon Baker Scholarship Fund in honor of her son. As an extraordinarily gifted woman ZaVonda is an entrepreneur in every sense of the word. Today she is still the owner of ZaVonda's Hair & More; however, she has stepped out on faith and birthed even greater. She is the CEO of *T.I.T.S & T.I.R.E.S.*, a business that reminds us to trust in the word of God, Trust In Things Said; in addition, to her own venture Ms. ZaVonda is nurturing her youngest daughter, Tracie Hockaday, in her business, I AM TOOUKY.

Last but not least ZaVonda is also using her gift of influence as the Promotions Coordinator for Emanuel Productions. Vonda explained to me that the name T.I.T.S & T.I.R.E.S. was given to her a few years ago, but at that time it didn't have a meaning. One day, the Lord put it on her heart to share her testimony, and at that moment the Lord gave her the meaning behind the name. Committed to encouraging youth everywhere her greatest desires is for them to know who they are, so they will never focus on who they are not. Bringing hope and creativity to another person's dream is another one of her amazing abilities, she is incredible at helping others in their business ventures as well.

ZaVonda Parrish is a single mother of four children and is a devoted member of Destiny Worship Center under the leadership of Pastor Tara Owens. When it comes to friendship ZaVonda is the most genuine she and I have had a friendship that has lasted for almost twenty-four years. We have worked together on many projects, programs, and fundraisers and no matter the occasion she gives every task her very best. She is a woman of God, a woman of purpose and much like the eagles that soar in the sky that's what I believe ZaVonda is doing in this season of her life, soaring. While walking into her destiny, she has never forgotten her past; instead, she uses the memory of her yesterday to catapult her into everything that God has in store for her. Witnessing her growth is incredible; I have no doubt that with her faith, her knowing who she is in Christ, with her drive, her good character, and her selflessness she has all of the ingredients to be a Godly leader and that's precisely who ZaVonda Vinson Parrish is becoming, daily.

Patricia Brown holding her great niece ZaVonda.

I SURRENDER ALL

"I believe laundry is the only thing that should be separated by color."- **ZaVonda Vinson Parrish**

ZaVonda and F   Give a man a fish and he will starve, Teach a man
                 to fish he will eat forever.

Trust In Things Said

"For I am not ashamed of the gospel, because it is the power of God that brings salvation to everyone who believes: first to the Jew, then to the Gentile. For the gospel reveals the righteousness of God that comes by faith from start to finish, just as it is written: The righteous will live by faith." — **Romans 1:16-17**

"Some people won't like you because they can't figure you out; why are you still blessed after the things you used to do? When you are forgiven, God forgets about it. I'm not perfect...I'm just trying to find out what's behind the door that He is showing me." – ZaVonda Vinson Parrish

Tracie "Toouk" Hockaday

Tracie is the daughter of Zavonda Vinson Parrish and Tracey Hockaday. At the age of 12, she is currently one of the youngest CEOs in Amelia County—the name of her business is I AM TOOUKY. The purpose behind I AM TOOUKY is to connect and reach out to youth like her, to show them who they are and what they can do. Tracie is developing a clothing and apparel line that hopes to aide in raising low self-esteem, promote the end to bullying, and encourage all to stop the violence. She, with the assistance of her supporters, has begun organizing events that she uses to show youth from ages 5-14 that they can become young CEOs as well. Through her life and her business, she is working to teach her peers that there is nothing that they can't accomplish and that NOW is the time for them to start making their dreams come true. Each item that is produced by I Am TOOUKY has a space where positive words can be written; youth can tell their own stories by writing and proclaiming who they are! So far her company has produced shirts, shorts, drinkware and so much more; the best part about it is that each of these items are teaching tools. It teaches our children to speak positively over themselves and to know who God says they are. By giving youth the ability to fill in their own space they in turn take control of their own destiny and tell the world I AM whatever I can dream to be. Tracie's first event the I AM TOOUKY Extravaganza was wonderfully organized and was hosted by another youth entrepreneur, Ms. Imani Crawley. Five youth speakers spoke on why and how they started their businesses; we were entertained by a young rapper known as Prince Sauce Jr. who performed fearlessly; and lastly, we received words of encouragement by Minister Emanuel Hyde III. Zavonda Vinson Parrish and her mother Annie Parrish also stood to give the youth words of encouragement. Overall, this extravaganza not only inspired youth but the adults who were in attendance as well; everything was truly a blessing, not to mention the food and the decor were immaculate. Without question, Tracie "Toouk" Hockaday is a trailblazer and a business mogul in the making.

For more information check out her website, *Ebonyroseexpressions.com/affiliates-sponsored/i-am-toouky/*, which is sponsored by Ebony Brown

Tanesha Delaney

Unstoppable & Covered

Tanesha Delaney is the daughter of Mary Delaney and the late Herbert Trueheart. In 2012, she achieved her goal of graduating from Virginia Commonwealth University with a Bachelor of Science Degree. God has placed a desire in her to help young girls and young ladies, who have negative perspectives about their self-worth, to develop a different and more positive way of looking at themselves. She understands very well that life brings its challenges and many times things will happen in life that we have no control over. Acutely aware, that young women and young girls, make decisions that in hindsight they have come to regret BUT what they may not know is that does not diminish their value—they are still treasures. God has given this young woman a vision when it comes to helping to promote self-worth amongst girls, teens, and other young women like herself, and that vision is Treasure. She, through the grace of God, is beginning to develop this vision; its mission is to help young girls and young ladies to build a keen understanding of their worth—to assist them in recognizing their importance, why they matter, and who God says they are.

Every product that will be released through Treasure is meant first to inform and then to serve as a constant reminder to every girl, and every woman that she is irreplaceable, necessary, capable, powerful, and beautiful within. Treasure is deeply devoted to always standing as a reminder that regardless of what a person's story might be, and irrespective of who or what that don't have, they are significant. Tanesha says, "I am convinced that the value a girl places on herself while she is young will play a role in the choices that she makes, the things she chooses to do, and what she will or will not accept as she grows into womanhood." Therefore, it is imperative that we help our young girls and ladies develop an accurate view of their self-worth. That is everything that Treasure stands for. Tanesha will be fully launching this vision in the near future; in the meantime, while she is hard at work seeking God's guidance, she is also using this time to allow Him to reveal to her all of the undiscovered treasures that she carries.

She has learned that God as the ability to love you past anything, love you out of anything, and love you in spite of everything. There is nothing that you've done so wrong that His love won't forgive; at the end of the day God is just waiting for us to choose him. He wants to show us the treasures that we carry. With certainty, Tanesha says, "One treasure that I know I carry within me, is Him. God is one of my treasures...He is my good thing. My hope is that every girl and every young woman would know that same truth." When you start knowing that for yourself, and you begin to seek God for everything, you become unstoppable.

Min. Emanuel Hyde III

An Unconquered Soul

I am the son of Elder Emanuel A. Hyde Jr. and Betty Minter Hyde. I was born on October 16, 1980, in Richmond, VA. I grew up in a Christian home with awesome parents and two older sisters. My father and mother have always been hard working and have given all they could for their family. My aunts and uncles also had a hand in my upbringing, and I have always been very close to my first cousins, many of them are more like my brothers and sisters. I attended both Richmond and Amelia County Public Schools; however, I graduated from high school in Amelia in 1999. During my middle and high school years in Amelia, I joined the school chorus and participated in several talent shows in Virginia. While in eighth grade I received fourth place in the Virginia All-District Chorus, representing Amelia County. I was also active in the Junior R.O.T.C. I can recall performing a song, that I wrote, at the first Military Ball held at the Amelia high school, the song was entitled "A Chance." I often tell people that I was raised in the church and that is the truth. My parents were very active in the church so since I was a baby going there has been a part of my life. When I was only four years old, my aunt Rev. Shirley Stuart led me to Christ in my parent's living room. Although I was very young, I can still remember a lot of what she said. In 1985, I joined the First Independent Methodist Church under the leadership of Bishop John L. Harris Sr.

I first felt the presence of God in the spring of 1986 while visiting my adopted grandmother, Maggie Thornton, in King William VA. One day I was walking in the field at her home when I began to feel a presence upon me. The next thing I knew I was preaching my first sermon in that field; for years after that experience I would often, in my childhood, preach to my family, friends, and classmates. Since the age of six, I was always in a choir beginning with the First Independent Methodist Church Youth Choir and later the Crusade for Christ Christian Church Ministries Youth Choir. In 1992, I attended the Amelia County Sunday School Christmas choir rehearsals; the choir director was Rev. Ralland V. Robinson, and the pianist was Elwood Royal Jr. Reverend Robinson selected me to lead a song with his son, Ralland Robinson Jr., and that song was entitled "How Excellent." He asked me to sing that song during the Christmas program, and I did; the spirit of God moved so powerfully while I was singing and since that day I began to lead songs at church whenever asked. During the 1990s I joined several groups and choirs which included: God's Heavenly Ones, New Vision, Liberty Baptist Church Choir, and The Heavenly Voices (founded by Sean Archer, Richard Jefferson, and John Holman). In the early 2000's I joined the Mt. Olive Male Chorus, and the Center Union Choir where I also helped out with the Senior Choir.

For a time I battled health challenges, and at one point things became very critical with me, but the Lord completely healed my body and gave me another chance at life. After recovering from poor health things began to go well for me, then because of decisions that I made my life began to take a turn for the worse. I first started drinking and experimenting with drugs early on in my life; I believe it was a way of rebelling against my upbringing, I wanted to do things my way, and I tried to fit in with the crowd. From 2008—2009 I recorded several songs and worked with producers DeVon Jones and Christopher Jefferson on three secular songs called, I Need You Over, M.A.R.Y and Rock Star. Even though I am not proud of every lyric I wrote in those songs it was still an exciting experience to record and work with great talents such as DeVon Jones; each of us has come a long way, today DeVon is a minister of the Gospel. However, from 2005 until 2009 I made reckless decisions which caused me to eventually became addicted to alcohol and drugs. Consuming alcohol took a toll on me, and I began to drink independently and not just socially. For a while, my life was out of control, and I had some close calls but I am thankful to God for his keeping power. I've been in accidents but praise God that I was never seriously injured. One wrong decision can make a permanent impact on your life. Although I was never incarcerated for an extended period, I have seen the inside of a jail several times for making poor decisions. It was those experiences that led me to answer the call that is upon my life. I will never forget, in 2009, I felt like I was at rock bottom while staying in Richmond at a friend's house, I decided one Sunday morning that I needed to hear God's word. I left the house and ended up at New Birth Ministries; Rev. Ralland Robinson, who is the founder and pastor over this church, preached a sermon called, "Tell the devil, I've Changed my mind." The following Sunday I went to my home church, Crusade for Christ Christian Church Ministries and the Nathaniel Robinson Memorial Choir was singing a song called, "Let Go, Let God." My former pastor, Bishop John L. Harris Sr., looked in the back of the church and before he started to preach, he said: "Let it go Scoop." That day the sermon that Bishop gave was entitled, "You Ran well, but who hindered you from Obeying the Truth?" After the sermon was over, I ran to the front of the church and rededicated my life to God and over time God delivered me from drugs and alcohol.

From the time I rededicated my life to the Lord, my life has not been the same. The wrong I was doing became uncomfortable, and the chains that had me spiritually bound began to break. I learned from those experiences that God will finish what he started in your life. It does not matter how low you have been or what you have done, Jesus can pick you up and make your life brand new. While in my process of deliverance, the first thing I had to do was overcome people, what they thought and the things they said. People always have a way of holding other people to their past or what they think they know about them. I had to get a so what attitude no matter what anyone said because God had given me another chance and forgave me of my sins. In return, I had to forgive myself, especially for the years of addictions and self-destruction. I finally surrendered to the call of God and accepted that He chose me to be a Minister, to reach the unreachable through his word because that is what he did for me. After officially returning to Crusade for Christ Christian Church Ministries I joined the Combined Choir, and in November 2010 I joined the Nathaniel Robinson Male Chorus, under the leadership of James Conyers. The group of men within that male chorus was a blessing to me; they helped cultivate me into who I am today. Those chorus members were: James Conyers, the late Deacon Silas Jones, Keith Conner, Bro. Gus Williams, Bus, the late Richard Robbins, Richard Adams and others. In 2011, I joined a group called Grateful under the leadership of Richmond's first black city council woman, Michelle Mosby. This group was made up of men and women who gave glory to God through their song. We would sing at community events, church services, and anniversaries. On one occasion Grateful was asked to minister at the Chesterfield Women's Diversion Center where my brother-in-Christ, Pastor Uzziah Harris was delivering the word. We experienced the power of God in such a remarkable way lives were changed that evening. In 2014 I had a great desire to be baptized again; to go down in the watery grave was symbolic of what the Lord was doing in my life. I knew when I came out of the water I wouldn't be the same, that I would leave my past there and I would be ready for what was to come. I asked my brother in Christ, Pastor Lee Day, to baptize me, although I was not a member of his church, he agreed; I was baptized in June 2014. From 2014-2015, I began visiting Destiny Worship Center (DWC) worship services and bible study, and it was in 2015 that I joined under the leadership of Pastor Tara Owens and Deacon Tony Owens; I started to grow further in God and began to see who I was in Christ in Jesus. It was through this ministry that I learned the true meaning of servanthood and on July 30, 2017, I became a licensed minister, and I'm currently a Youth Minister at DWC. I desire to reach the masses, primarily the youth through my testimony and my ministry. I want to reach those who feel like life isn't worth living or the one that feels as if they can't change. I know that the Lord can pick up, clean up and use them for His Glory if they allow him to. I am single, saved and try each day to live what I sing and preach about. I want my life to exemplify Christ in all I say and do from now until I die; all of my baggage is now over board, and now I am ready for my destiny. If it had not been for the grace and mercy of God I would not be here today; the Lord has made a significant change in my life and every day for me is a day of opportunity to give him the glory and honor.

I'm not sure what the future holds for me, but I do know that my future will be far better than past. I've learned through God's word, I've learned who I am and what I can do; for it is written in Philippians 4:13, I can do all things through Christ who strengthens me. I AM EMANUEL. I AM SAVED. I AM DELIVERED. I AM SET FREE. I AM GOD'S CHILD, AND NOW I AM A KING!

"For whom the Son has set free, is free indeed." — **John 8:36**

The Elevation Service of Emanuel Hyde III

Min. Emanuel and Rosetta Broadnax   Deacon Tony, Pastor, Min. Emanuel and Min.Towana

Torrie Patterson sings   Evang. Shirley A. Stuart (aunt)   Elder and Mrs. E.A. Hyde Jr.

Pastor Tara & Minister   Allison Owens   Min. E.A. Hyde III and ZaVonda   Pastor Rachelle Tabb

Every since I was as a child, I was always been inquisitive about history, particularly African American History. I can recall many of the older people in the Red Lodge and Brick Church community of Amelia telling me stories of long ago. Little did I know I would be researching and writing about the people that the elderly had once told me of. In the early 1990's, Howard Hyde Jr. one of the first known historians for the Hyde family showed me how to look up records at the Amelia Courthouse. In essence, that day was the first time I was introduced to what would become a part of my life's work. In 2012, I began learning genealogy, and with the help of Janice Gentry, Garland Ervin, Carolyn Carroll and others I learned how to analyze DNA and find out more about my ancestral heritage. It was within that year when I wrote my first book "Securing the history of the Eldridge – Minter family." In 2013, while researching the Red Lodge Community, which is also known as Tyler's, I decided to go to the Amelia County Courthouse to look up the slave owner of the land, Sen. William S. Archer. Little did I know I would soon find his will and slave inventory list which had fifty-five names on it. I researched each slaves name and their descendants; after two years of research, I found over 2,000 descendants of the Red Lodge Community who can be found nationwide. In fact, I am a descendant of a slave from that list whose name is Nancy Brown, the mother of Jennie Jones Hyde. From these findings, I later went on to write my second book, "Red Lodge and Its Connections." Since then I have researched my paternal grandmother's lineage and found many relatives.

On January 3, 2015, I was a part of a small but impactful movement in Sanford, NC. Through my research and with the help of several family members and neighbors of the Osgood and Colon community, I spoke out against the coal ash that was being dumped near my ancestor's grave site and my family's neighborhood. I appeared on the front page of the Sanford-Herald Newspaper in North Carolina for my research on the issue. Recently, I was informed that the efforts I made along with Sanford's NAACP, Stacy McBryde, Terica Luxton, Environmental, and my cousins Garland Ervin and Cardelia Hunt motivated Duke Energy to cease the plans of dumping coal ash in that vicinity. I also was featured in the Amelia Bulletin Monitor, in 2016, about genealogy research and the second book that I published, "Red Lodge and Its Connections." God blessed me to release a third book entitled, "Moseley Echoing Winds Whispers Messages from the Past." I have helped many families trace their heritage, and several of them have had the opportunity to unite with their distant relatives whose ancestors were separated through slavery. It is by God that two of my books have been accepted into the Library of Virginia and the Library of Ohio. I desire to preserve African American history worldwide and to educate the young and the old on our history. I'm thankful for all that has been done so far, and all the Lord has allowed me to accomplish. However, one thing is for sure, it takes a team to make a dream a reality. In January 2018, the Lord blessed me with a vision to become the founder and President of a company called, Emanuel Productions. Within weeks the Lord showed me that Tanesha Delaney was to be Vice President of Emanuel Productions and ZaVonda Vinson Parrish was to be the Media Coordinator. Since that time God has blessed every work we have set out to do; I am honored that these ladies agreed to work along with me. The purpose behind Emanuel Productions is to empower all people with the love of God so that they might know their worth as Kingdom citizens. We desire to preserve the legacy of African American history not only within Amelia but the entire state of Virginia as well as North Carolina. We stand firmly on the expression, *how can you understand where you are going in your future if you don't appreciate your past*? It is understood that each of us stands on another person's shoulders; so, we are committed to acknowledging the African Americans who have helped to pave the way for us today.

Emanuel Productions

Together we are rising to a platform to preserve the history of the African American people for generations to come.

President & Vice President

Media Coordinator & President

President: Emanuel Hyde III

Vice President: Tanesha Delaney

Media Productions/Stylist: ZaVonda V. Parrish

Contact Us: (804) 625-1661

Email: Emanuelproductions18@gmail.com

Cover Design: Emanuel Hyde III

Author: Emanuel Hyde III

Editor: Tanesha Delaney

Book Promotions: ZaVonda Vinson Parrish

We Honor

The Memory of the late Mrs. Annie Mondrey

Mr. Lester and the late Thelma Randall

The Memory of the late Dr. Henry Featherston

Mrs. Evelyn Harris

Deacon Henry Foster

Mrs. Shirley Wade

Deacon Elwood and Vernell Royall Sr.

All of the information you have given me has blessed this book tremendously, this book would not be complete id it wasn't for these individuals that are past and present.

"The Last Shall Be First"

ZaVonda Vinson Parrish, Tanesha Delaney, Min. Emanuel Hyde III

This book is dedicated to the loving memory

of

Ms. Sylvia Archer

(September 30, 1950 – March 21, 2018)

Thank you for all of your love and support down through the years. You will never be forgotten.

Continue to Rest In Peace Sivi!

Acknowledgements

First of all, I would like to thank God for life, and the ability to complete all of what He wants me to do. It is in Him, and through Him that I live move and have my being. I am thankful for how He is keeping me. My life is not my own, all that I have done and everything I do is all for your glory Lord. To God be the Glory!

To my parents Elder Emanuel Jr. and Betty Hyde thank you for raising me to be the gentleman I am. Thank you for believing in me when others doubted me; for supporting me even when you may not have understood. I love and appreciate you both. To my sisters Marshae Minter and Dee Dee Anderson; and to my niece, Brittaney N. Anderson thank you, ladies, for being consistent in supporting me. Love you all.

To my Spiritual Leaders, Pastor Tara Owens and Deacon Tony Owens, thank you both for always being the support system that I need. Thank you for Godly leadership, prayers, and encouragement— the two of you are indeed heaven sent. Also, to Assistant Pastor Katie Herbert, Rev. Shirley Jefferson, Deacon Central Jefferson, Min. Marquis Carlisle, Minister Shanice Carlisle, and the entire Destiny Worship Center family I'd like to thank you all for your love and support. DWC Church family, I thank God that I am a part of your lives.

To the Emanuel Productions team; Tanesha Delaney, there is no way I can thank you for all you have done and all that you do. Your dedication to our God-given assignment does not go unnoticed. You have traveled with me and helped me to make this a success, I truly appreciate you. ZaVonda Vinson Parrish – we have been working together for many years and most of all we are friends. Thanks for all you do to make sure the team looks great for all events. Thank you for always pushing me and just being yourself. You are awesome sis, and I love the you that God created. Thanks for using your promotional skills to get the word out. No man is an island, and I know that I could not have asked for a more magnificent team. This is God's doing, and I thank God for the connection. You both are truly an added blessing in my life, and I want you both to know that you inspire me in so many ways. This is the work the Lord has put in our hands. We have done this together, and I know that eyes haven't seen neither have ears heard, the things that the Lord has in store for us. It is our winning season individually and collectively.

To all of my aunts and uncles: Irene White, John and Dr. Sandra Seay, Sarah Davis, Charles and Blanche Hyde Jefferson; Willie and Anna Marie Bowers, Melvin and Rev. Shirley A. Stuart, Carolyn and Henry Carroll; Howard Hyde Jr. and Lynnette Hyde, Lonnie and Mary Harris, Clinton and Virginia Hyde; Clyde and Delois Hyde, Dr. Cleo Davis, and Yvonne Davis thanks for all you have done for me. Minister Amber Davidson thank you for your consistent prayers and support. To my Godmother Maxine Hernandez, your prayers are always felt. To Bishop John L. Harris Sr. and the past & present members of the Crusade for Christ Christian Church Ministries thanks for your love and encouragement. To all of many cousins The Hyde, Granger, Kelly, Jones, Goode, Lewis, Eldridge, Minter, Long, Sledge, Johnson, Robinson, Hicks, and Person families I love you all. Thanks to Lester Randall, Deacon Frank B. Tyler, Jr., the Russell Grove Alumni Association, the Amelia Historical Society, Chermine Booker, Gloria Robinson, Mrs. Thelma Conyers, Barry Archer, Sylvia Hicks, Sylvia Gray, Daphne Holman, Deacon Elwood Royal, Mary Person, JoVan Holman, Antoine Jackson, Mrs. Annie Mondrey, Mary Jasper, Maxine Mondrey, Ebony Brown, Clementine Harris Marilyn Hicks, Louise Harris, Dea. Garland Montague, Chester Grove Baptist Church, LaTasha Moon, Mrs. Sarah Delaney, Chris Archer, Mrs. Evelyn Harris, Racell Broadnax, Rosetta Broadnax, Shirley Jackson, Lorraine Broadnax, Ricky Broadnax, Edwin Wilson, Reytina Banks, La'Toya Person, Shiccorey Garrrett, Mrs. Lois Mondrey, James Conyers, Jamir Williamson, Deacon Elwood and Vernell Royall, Stephen Brown, Rev. Anna Bates, Shante Meyers, and Charilda Thompson Harper and everyone that helped make this written work a success. May God bless you all.

Advertisment

Ebony Rose Expressions, LLC

Please choose Ebony Rose Expressions, LLC to create a custom item for whatever your need may be. Let's learn how to create together.

Printed Shirts, mugs etc. available on her website

https://ebonyroseexpressions.com/

Contact: ebonyroseexpressions@outlook.com

Clementine Harris

Owner and operator of Total Lifestyle in Amelia, VA. She is an independent contractor at Herbalife.

Check out her site
http://www.goherbalife.com/clementinemitchell/en-us

Tomeka Parrish

Owner and operator of Renew II

(804) 601-0943

Made in the USA
Middletown, DE
11 March 2022

62337055R00108